How to
Really Help Your
Teenager

Presented with love by the
BARBARA BARRINGTON JONES
Family Foundation

How to **Really** Help Your Teenager

BARBARA BARRINGTON JONES & BRAD WILCOX

DESERET
BOOK

SALT LAKE CITY, UTAH

Part of the proceeds from this book will be used to benefit the youth programs on the Brigham Young University campuses.

Library of Congress Cataloging-in-Publication Data

Jones, Barbara Barrington.
    Straight Talk for Parents: what teenagers wish they could tell you / by
Barbara Barrington Jones and Brad Wilcox.
        p.   cm.
    Includes index.
    ISBN 0–87579–819–5
        1. Parent and teenager. 2. Social work with teenagers. I. Wilcox, Brad. II. Title.
HQ799.15.J66 1993
306.874—dc2093–39919
                                                                        CIP

Printed in the United States of America
10   9   8   7   6   5   4   3

To Hal Jones

Contents

Preface

Working with teenagers under any circumstance is challenging. Young people can often cause a lump in the throat—and, just as often, they can cause a pain in the neck. If we were with you right now, we'd sing a song that says, "With God, nothing is impossible"—not that we have such great voices, but because we believe the message of the song.

Let us tell you about one of our friends. A few years ago this young man's rough lifestyle might be described as "the before picture." There was not a commandment he had not struggled with, a family member he had not hurt in one way or another. His parents, true and faithful members of the Church, had tried everything, but each line they drew, he crossed over; each ultimatum they gave was meaningless to him.

Late at night in the quiet of their room, the parents told each other, "When he was just a little boy, things were so different." They remembered when he was sweet and valiant. They chuckled as they recalled how he would march fearlessly to the front of the chapel to bear his testimony. He used to tell total strangers on the street that he was going to be a missionary. He used to tell smokers he saw that they were going to die if they didn't repent. When he had questions, he used to look to his parents for answers. He used to hug them and tell them he loved them. Now he wouldn't even come close to them.

Pornography, vandalism, wild parties—the list went on and on. Finally another parental line was drawn. He was told that he absolutely must be home by a certain time. Commitments were made and consequences outlined. Things were going as planned until one night, when he did not arrive at the scheduled time. Two o'clock arrived and then three and then four. Finally the father decided his son had gone too far. In the darkness, he went to the back door and, just as he had warned his son, he locked it.

No sooner had he done so than he received a strong impression that he should unlock the door. "No," he argued with himself. "My son knows this is coming. If I back down now, he'll never believe me again when I lay down any law. I have to do this for his sake. It's the only way I can help him." Still the impression was clear. Finally he unlocked the door, muttering, "If my son is going to leave home, it will never be because I locked him out."

In the morning, it was obvious by the trail of clothing down the stairs to the son's room that he had come home. The family went about preparing breakfast when he suddenly appeared in the doorway and asked if he could speak with his father alone. The two of them went into another room, where the father expected to hear the same old excuses and rationalizations. But before he could say anything, his son said, "Dad, I know you said you would lock the door if I was ever late again. When I came home and found it open, you will never know what that meant to me." The words caught the father off guard. This was not what he had expected to hear. "Last night," the boy went on, "I wasn't out with my friends. I was out all alone. I was"—he paused—"I was praying, and I haven't done that for a long time."

The father couldn't believe what he was hearing. His son spoke of how unhappy he had been and of the changes he was going to make. He said, "When I found the door open, I knew that you hadn't given up on me." The father could hardly speak. He simply offered a silent prayer thanking his Heavenly Father for guiding him to unlock a door he had already locked on that crucial night.

Did the young man's humble attitude last, or was it just a momentary thing? Soon after this, he was called by an inspired bishop to be the first assistant in the priests quorum. He later served a mission, and now he is teaching full-time seminary. With God's help, nothing is impossible.

There are other stories too. It isn't easy for us as parents and leaders to know how we should act and feel when teenagers aren't acting up to their potential, no matter how great or small the offense. Sure, we proceed with all the self-control and positive attitudes we can muster, but deep down we feel resentment, even anger at times, because of how they are treating us. We don't even like them for being so thoughtless and uncaring. We resent being expected to give them the attention and time they demand. Then we are angry with ourselves because we know we shouldn't feel that way about them.

Now may we tell you another friend of ours. Even at 13, this boy had made some decisions that had led him down the wrong path and off the deep end. He was the age of a Scout, but he had given up being trustworthy, loyal, helpful, friendly, courteous, and all the other virtues Scouts are expected to exemplify. He painted his room black. His hair, clothes, language, and music became wilder. His parents didn't know what to do. They consulted with his teachers, school and professional counselors, their bishop. But they couldn't get through to him. He rejected the help being offered on all sides. Years passed, and he grew larger and began threatening his younger brothers and sisters. His parents were seriously considering evicting him from their home.

Then a youth leader—someone who didn't even know him the way he was before—showed up one day at the park where the boy was skateboarding. The leader showed sincere interest in the young man's agility on the skateboard. "You ought to enter a competition," he told him. "You're good enough to win. In fact, you could do demonstrations for people who want to learn some of the tricks you do." This was the door-opening experience his parents and bishop had prayed for. This was the personal attention and caring that counselors had not delivered. From that point on, things started to change.

Then they found out there had been some abuse—a neighbor had molested the boy. After it had happened, the boy felt that it was somehow his own fault. He couldn't face himself, so he started to run away to all the destructive things he could find. For years, he ran so hard and fast that no one could catch him. No one except a leader who was willing to do it with a skateboard.

Now this young man and his parents are working through their past together. His bedroom is not black anymore, but painted light blue. The music he listens to now is from tapes found in LDS bookstores. He is attending early morning seminary faithfully. Recently he bore his testimony in church. "I love the Savior," he declared. "I love my family. I can't wait for my mission. I can't think of anything I would rather do than serve a mission and help others." With God's help, nothing is impossible.

As parents and leaders, we usually see better than young people the ends of the roads they are on. But while we may warn and teach, we still have to watch as they do things their own way. We may even have to pick up the pieces at times. There are times when we may feel completely helpless. We may wonder how best to approach the subject, and a sense of paralysis may set in when we do not know what to do. Should we show more love, or should we discipline more firmly? Should we try to understand and help in a constructive way, or should we do nothing at all and experience self-anger as a consequence?

One so-called expert says we should enforce rules consistently or our children will turn out wrong, while another says that unless we let things go and lighten up, our children will turn out warped and impossible to change. Then, no matter what we try, expert and nonexpert alike line up to point out the errors and say, "I told you so."

When we look at teenagers, we need to remember that inside those physically maturing bodies are little children. It is never too late to make a difference in the lives of young people we care about. Whatever the situation of the teenagers in our lives—whether they are struggling through the trials that are normal and common to their teenage years or are getting caught up in the worldliness all about them—they need help.

In a general conference talk in April 1992, President Gordon B. Hinckley quoted an address by Senator Dan Coats of Indiana, who said, "The challenges to the health and well-being of America's youth are not primarily rooted in illness or economics. Unlike the past, the problem is not childhood disease or unsanitary slums. The most basic cause of suffering . . . is profoundly self-destructive behavior. Drinking. Drugs. Violence. Promiscuity. A crisis of behavior and belief. A crisis of character."

Counseling groups, drug rehabilitation centers, government education programs, and encounter-type programs—the list of agencies and programs committed to helping youth seems endless. But what about religion? What about God? While some acknowledge a nebulous and non-denominational "higher power," most smugly consider those who ask such questions as uneducated at best and hopelessly fanatical at worst.

Many do not see religion as a solution or even a help. In fact, churches are often seen as the narrow-minded guilt-imposing causes of problems.

How should we as parents and leaders help our teenagers? How does the Lord help? "The Lord works from the inside out. The world works from the outside in," according to President Ezra Taft Benson. "The world would mold men by changing their environment. Christ changes men, who then change their environments." Unless we deal with the deeper needs that drive one student to quitting, another to eating disorders, and someone else to drinking, our efforts will only be of temporary assistance. The same goes for less serious challenges, such as making poor choices in music, having a messy room, and not doing homework. Positive changes that we get, force, or make may not last when we are no longer there to control the external circumstances.

To talk about vandalism, theft, running away, bad friends, pornography, and dysfunctional homes is to avoid facing the real issues. Most observable negative behaviors are usually strategies young people use to deal with deeper problems, such as low self-esteem, poor communication skills, inability to cope with stress and pressure, and weak spirituality. In order to really help teenagers to solve and overcome their problems, we must first discover what is causing the problems and then address those underlying factors.

Some time ago we were asked to develop a series of classes for Education Week at Brigham Young University on how parents and leaders can better understand and help teenagers. Our main qualifications were that we have spent many years in working with teenagers through the Church's youth programs, and that we are also parents and speak from personal experience in our own homes.

As we prepared for this assignment, we conducted an informal survey among teenagers. We distributed forms at youth conferences and other youth programs and through missionary acquaintances in other areas. More than a thousand teenagers in 38 states and 10 countries responded.

In the following chapters, we present information gleaned from the comments of these young people. Based on their comments and our own experiences with youth, we give you some specific suggestions, and strategies to help teenagers feel good about themselves, deal with stress, and strengthen their testimonies. Why? Because as parents and leaders ourselves, we care—and we want to do whatever we can to help you and to make a difference in teenagers' lives.

Acknowledgments

We are grateful to our spouses, Hal Jones and Debi Wilcox, who believe in us and believed that this book could become a reality. We thank them for allowing us to dream and giving us time—between the daily work, responsibilities, and routines of life—to pursue our dreams. We acknowledge their sacrifice, support, and never-failing love, and recognize their wisdom in "telling it like it is" when they read our rough drafts. We also appreciate our children for their patience, for allowing us to make our mistakes, and for allowing us to share some of those personal lessons in this book.

We are grateful to Val C. and Ray T. Wilcox for reviewing, editing, and revising the manuscript; Janet Thomas, Kris Mackay, Louise Jackson, and Laurie Petty for their contributions as writers; and Lorie O'Toole and Sonja Wasden for the endless hours of typing, mailing, organizing, and compiling, as well as personal support. We thank Shane Adamson and Linda Otte for their assistance in researching references.

We express appreciation to Larry Dietz, Ph.D., for professional expertise and direction; Earl Leroy and Mary Lois Gunnell for reviewing the manuscript and offering valuable suggestions; and Robert E. and Helen Wells, Clark and Julie Smith, Kenneth and Kathy Cope, Kirk and Gretchen Jensen, Gerald Hinckley, Cynthia Abrea, and Judy Tobin for encouraging us to write.

We are grateful to Ron Hills, Glen McClure, Susan Overstreet, and John Bytheway at the BYU-Provo campus, Teresa Bigbie and Dona Brown at the BYU-Hawaii campus, and all who work with CES Youth and Family Programs for the opportunities they have allowed us to learn, grow, and serve. Proceeds from this book will be used to benefit these wonderful programs, which influence so many young people for good. Thanks also to Mack Palmer and Ellen Allied, who felt the need and first invited us to prepare a series at BYU's Education Week for parents and youth leaders on helping teenagers.

Eleanor Knowles, our good friend and editor, pushed us until we had a manuscript we could be proud of. We also thank Sheri Dew, Patricia Parkinson, and other staff members at Deseret Book, and Steve Wasden, who helped in conceptualizing the initial design.

Finally, thanks to the wonderful and enthusiastic counselors and speakers at the BYU youth programs. They are constant examples for us. Thanks as well to the dedicated parents and youth leaders around the Church with whom we have visited and with whom we have planned, laughed, and cried. We appreciate the valiant and strong young people with whom we have met and worked, especially those who allowed us to use their stories, insights, photographs, and words of advice in this book. They have taught us much.

We are proud of the love the youth feel for the Savior and his restored gospel, and compliment them on the standards they are living and the wonderful choices they are making. We hope they will always feel our personal support and love.

God bless you all.

PART ONE

Understanding Teenagers

CHAPTER 1

Sources of Self-esteem

Low self-esteem, which is prevalent among teenagers, paralyzes them and keeps them from doing positive things with their lives. In order to help our youth, we need to know what aspects of their lives need attention so that we can help them build their self-esteem. How can we recognize when teenagers have a problem with self-esteem? What are the main sources of self-esteem in their lives?

"I feel so inadequate, so inferior, so average. I watch and study everyone around me—people, pictures in magazines, actresses, everyone—picking out every feature that I wish I could have for myself. In every person I see a trait that I rip myself apart for not having or for not being able to do as well. Jealousy has made me a depressed and hopeless person. I am overweight. My hair's a mess. My eyebrows are each different. My eyelashes grow every direction. My nose is long—even my mother would admit this, because she has the same one, only not quite as bad."

 S ing us a song," the young people were calling to a girl in their group. We were at a youth conference where teenagers were putting on a spur-of-the-moment talent show as they waited for the dance to begin. Some young women sang and a few young men told jokes and did impersonations. Now they were coaxing one of the young women to sing. "Come on, you have a great voice," they said. "Sing the song we learned at camp."

We could see the young sister's embarrassment. Everyone

began to feel uncomfortable. Brad quickly got some of the young men to stand up and sing "I Hope They Call Me on a Mission" and "Popcorn Popping on the Apricot Tree," complete with actions. The entire group was laughing and involved. No one noticed Barbara as she sought out the embarrassed girl. Barbara asked, "Is everything all right?"

"I hate it when my friends do that," the girl replied.

"They were just trying to make you feel good."

"I'm a horrible singer," the girl said angrily. "If I got up there, I would totally bomb."

Barbara didn't say any more. She simply listened as the girl's feelings came gushing out. "I can't do anything right. I'm ugly and fat and I'm the dumbest person in my school."

Just then some of the stake leaders called to Barbara and the girl to come be in some pictures.

The girl stood up and started to leave the room. Barbara said, "Don't go. Come stand by me. I would love to have a picture with you."

"No one wants a picture of me," was the response. "I wish cameras had never been invented. I hate pictures." The girl hurried out of the room, and as Barbara watched her leave, she sensed that the real message had very little to do with hating cameras.

Self-esteem is the mental picture we have of ourselves, the value we place on ourselves. Basically, it is how friendly we feel toward ourselves. Many young people struggle to maintain a high and positive self-esteem. When teenagers have healthy attitudes about themselves, it is much easier to overcome problems. Such people are sure of themselves and able to stand up to peer pressure. They do better in school, at church, and in all aspects of their lives.

Low self-esteem seems to paralyze young people and keep

them from doing the positive things that will give them the very confidence they lack. They are often vulnerable, unsure, and negative. They attempt to mask their insecurities by withdrawing or becoming braggarts or even violent bullies. Still, their insecurities are usually obvious. Research confirms that low self-esteem is related to poor mental health, poor academic achievement, and delinquency.

Barbara works with Dr. Larry Dietz, a psychiatrist who did his dissertation on self-esteem in adolescents. He has identified the following eight sources of self-esteem:

1. Social acceptance

In a large study of teenagers done at University of Wyoming, 71 percent said that "having a lot of friends" was most important to them. Social acceptance is a sense of belonging that is influenced by what others think and say about us. In addition to friends, teenagers are also influenced by the messages communicated by parents, teachers, relatives, and leaders. That seems pretty straightforward until you realize that what people are actually saying or thinking does not really affect self-esteem so much as what a teenager perceives is being said and thought.

Barbara was born and reared in Texas. She remembers hearing her Aunt Barbara, for whom she was named, saying such things about her as "Look at that girl's ears. They stick out like Dumbo's. I guess she's just naturally funny looking."

Barbara also remembers wearing a turquoise and white striped blouse and black skirt on the first day of fifth grade. As she was going out the front door, her mother commented, "Barbara, you have a figure just like a sausage."

The summer before Barbara entered seventh grade, she grew to the height she is today, five foot ten. "I changed schools that year," she remembers, "and there I was on the first day of school, walking through the halls just trying to get my arms and legs going in the same direction. I was trying to work the combination on my lock when the head cheerleader came around the corner, looked down at my feet, and exclaimed, 'Golly!' Then she ran around the corner and called to her friend, 'Kathy, get over here quick. Check out those feet!'"

Barbara had one friend all through school. Her name was Lynne, and she had the same height and build as Barbara. She also had big feet. They were nicknamed "the Bobsey Twins." They hated being taller than all the boys. Barbara's mother kept telling her, "Don't worry, the boys will grow," but Barbara says, "When we finally got to high school, they hadn't grown a bit. It was terrible."

Years later, Barbara's mother listened to one of Barbara's lectures and was surprised when Barbara told some of these stories. "Did I really say that you have a figure like a sausage?" she asked.

"Yes, you did," Barbara replied.

"Well, you know I really didn't mean it like that. I just meant that you didn't quite have a waistline." But that is not how Barbara heard her mother's comments.

"And I don't remember your Aunt Barbara saying that your ears stuck out like Dumbo's," Barbara's mother continued. But Barbara thought her ears stuck out like an elephant's, so she heard her Aunt Barbara's comments as validation of what she already believed about herself.

Finally, Barbara's mother said, "You were not five foot ten in the seventh grade. You didn't get that last spurt of height until you were entering high school."

Barbara said, "Mother, I felt as if I were six foot ten. All the boys and most of the girls were so much shorter. I tried slouching on one hip so I wouldn't feel so tall. I tried ducking my head down when I walked. My height was a problem I faced the whole time I was growing up." But the problem did not necessarily stem from how tall Barbara was so much as it stemmed from how she viewed herself.

Have you ever known a teenager who has worked hard all summer to buy new clothes for school, and someone at school asks, "Where did you get *that* outfit?"

If the person's self-esteem is high, he or she will say, "I like this outfit, and if you don't that's your problem." If not, he or she may never wear those clothes again, no matter how much they cost.

When Barbara speaks to teenagers, she asks them to raise their hands and vote on what they would do in the above situation. You guessed it. Virtually all of them say they would never wear that particular outfit again.

2. Performance

Self-esteem is also based on performance. Again, it is not actually how teenagers perform their work, but how they perceive they are doing.

Barbara's daughter once appeared in a beauty pageant in California. She was not selected as the winner. She was not one of the top finalists. However, she felt she had done her best. In a letter to the mother of another contestant, she wrote, "Thank you for sending me those pictures. I had a wonderful time at the pageant, and I hope your daughter did too. I learned so much, and even though I wasn't in the top ten, I know that I did my very best. I feel like a winner inside because I had the courage to try and I did all that I could." As this letter illustrates, self-esteem is usually not dependent upon winning so much as upon participating and doing one's best.

Brad attended a lecture at which the presenter said that to build self-esteem in students, teachers must find something in which each one could excel. "There has to be something that each person can do better than anyone else," he explained.

Brad disagreed. He later told the presenter that what he said was both unrealistic and unnecessary. Teenagers do not need to do things better than others in order to feel good about themselves. Self-esteem does not depend on trophies, high grades, money, or winning. Young people can get the same successful feelings when they know they have done something right and well. It might be nice to be number one in something, but that is not a requirement for self-esteem. Teenagers just need to feel they are trying and giving their best efforts.

Elder Robert E. Wells likes to quote an old Hindu proverb: "There is nothing noble in being superior to some other person— true nobility is in being superior to your own precious self."

3. The ability to discuss feelings

We often ask teenagers, "Can you discuss your feelings with adults?" Imagine parents confronting their son and saying, "We know that you took the family car without permission. We are really upset with you. You are not going to be able to use the car for two weekends."

But the young man knows he did not take the car—perhaps it was a brother or sister. If he can appropriately and calmly tell his parents, "Look, Mom and Dad, you are making a big mistake because I am telling you in all honesty that I did not take that car," then his self-esteem is high. But if he clams up, storms out, or marches off to his bedroom and slams the door behind him, then it is obvious that he has poor self-esteem.

One young woman told Brad about finally finding the courage to tell her father that she loved him. In the awkwardness of his emotions, the father said, "So which Sunday School teacher put you up to this little charade—or was it your seminary teacher?" The young woman was crushed. But instead of running off and wallowing in self-pity, she said, "Dad, that really hurts, because I wasn't doing this for seminary. I was doing it for you." She showed she had high self-esteem by being willing to discuss her feelings.

Barbara, her husband, and their two children are converts to the Church. When Barbara's son was on his mission, he wrote a letter to his father in which he shared his feelings. Barbara and her husband knew that their son's self-esteem was high when he wrote, "Thank you, Dad, for giving up alcohol after drinking for 40 years. That is an unforgettable testimony to me that we can perfect ourselves and get rid of bad habits. I feel that my worst habit is laziness, and I'm trying to conquer it. I *will* conquer it, just watch and see."

4. Opening up to others

Picture a room crowded with teenagers. First, we ask the young women, "Okay, ladies, pretend you're on a date with a guy and something really sensitive happens and tears start coming down his cheeks. What would you do?" By this time every young man in the room is tensing up and feeling embarrassed. But nearly all the young women sigh, and then one of them blurts out, "We like it when guys show their feelings."

Every time we try this little experiment with young people, we are amazed at the reaction of most of the young men. They are surprised. They have never dreamed that young women would understand.

At a testimony meeting during the Especially for Youth program, one young woman put it this way: "If young men cry at school, you think something is wrong—but if they cry in church, you know something is right."

Barbara tells young people, "If you can cry in front of your parents or a date, then your self-esteem is pretty high. If you hold everything in, you have some improving to do in this area."

5. The real versus the ideal

In today's world, young people are constantly barraged with ideals that are unreal. They can't turn around without another image of fitness, beauty, talent, and perfection being thrust upon them. Allen Litchfield, who speaks often to youth, points out that teenagers are going to feel defeated if they try to look as mature as those who portray teenagers on television and in movies. Most actors who play teenagers are between 25 and 35 years old.

Teenagers may wonder why they can't sing and dance the way people do on TV without getting worn out and winded. They don't realize that the music videos they watch are filmed over several days and that the performers are usually lip-synching because their dance routines are so challenging.

Magazine covers continually place pictures of the ideal before teens.

One magazine cover featuring the face of a popular movie star stated in the caption that this particular beauty needed "absolutely nothing." The following month, however, another magazine offered proof that even this beautiful star needed a little help. The retoucher's bill for the picture on the cover of the first magazine had been obtained, and it seems the beauty who needed "absolutely nothing" ran up a bill of $1,525 for retouching her photo.

We have found that though it is difficult, most young people are able to keep in perspective the pressures imposed by others. Some, however, have problems when they begin to internalize such expectations. When the ideal becomes self-imposed, we begin to hear comments like these: "I just have to get skinny or no one will like me and I won't get asked out," or "We have to win this game and make it to the play-offs or I'm going to die."

We sometimes ask young people to rate themselves on a scale of one to ten, with ten being the ideal. Most of them put themselves at five. That's normal and not terrible at all until the most significant people in their lives start insinuating, "That's not good enough. You have to be a ten, and it has to happen right now." We know of one young man whose grandmother told him, "You have to do better in school because I want you to be a success. I want you to be a doctor like your father and uncles. Your brothers didn't make it and none of your cousins made it. You're my last hope."

6. Physical well-being

Receiving our physical bodies is one of the main purposes of earth life. Even those who die in infancy, and who seem not to require any of the tests and experiences that we have, cannot progress without their bodies. When we recognize the eternal importance of our bodies, no wonder they present such constant challenges for us to maintain and deal with them. No wonder so many of our hardest temptations revolve around our physical selves.

Sometimes on the second day of a youth conference, Barbara

will begin her talk by saying, "You all feel great today, don't you? You feel rested and you've eaten well-balanced, nutritious meals, haven't you?" Of course, the teenagers are all groaning because they have stayed up all night talking and have eaten mostly junk food. How do they really feel? They feel terrible. We all know that same feeling too well.

Compare that feeling to what is expressed in a letter from a young man named Michael: "Before I went to youth conference, I was seriously thinking about suicide. I admit that something had to have been wrong with my head. It was probably a loose screw. I was unpopular in school, ate lunch alone, and was a little 'chunky' I also felt very depressed and unloved. Well, after youth conference, I decided to get rid of the sad, depressed me. I lost fifteen pounds and got a job. . . . Now I feel as if a fifty-pound jacket has been lifted off my back."

We are proud of this young man. He has made some positive changes in his life. He feels better and is more enthusiastic and in control of himself. As he has worked at being more fit physically, he has come to feel better about himself in other areas of his life as well.

7. Self comparison

Several years ago Barbara met a young man named Paul whose parents called her because she is an image consultant. They asked if they could fly their son out to California to work with her for a week. Barbara agreed, and so Paul came to stay in her home. At first they had conversations something like this:

"What do you like to do? Do you like sports?"

"No, I hate sports."

"How about school? Do you like school?"

"No, not really."

After several other similar exchanges, Barbara finally asked him, "What do you do when you get home from school?"

"Play the piano."

"What kind of things do you play?"

They went into the living room, where Paul sat at the piano and played a beautiful piece of music that he had composed. "Incredible!" Barbara exclaimed. "Look at the talent you have!"

"Yeah, but not like my brother," Paul replied. "He plays football." He then showed Barbara a picture of his brother—the muscular crew-cut captain of the high school football team. Paul was spending a lot of time comparing himself with his brother. He acted as if his piano playing were not important.

A first reaction in trying to help Paul feel better might have been to start pointing out the imperfections in his brother, but Barbara knew that trying to make others look smaller never makes us feel larger for long. Paul had to shine brightly by recognizing and cultivating his own gifts, not by dimming the lights around him.

Paul worked on overcoming his negative attitude about himself. He eventually served a mission. Not long after he returned, he sent Barbara the cover of his first recording—an entire album of original compositions, with a great-looking photo of Paul on the front. It was entitled "Paul Anderson: Himself."

8. Appearance

As much as we wish young people could realize that "the Lord looketh on the heart" (1 Samuel 16:7) and that the inside is what really counts, there is no escaping the fact that teenagers base much of their self-esteem on appearance. During adolescence, they are acutely aware of how they look. They agonize about their complexions and being over- or underweight. They can usually pinpoint a few things they like about how they look and then provide long, detailed lists of defects, real or imagined.

At a seminar in a public school, Barbara told some young women that she would help them if they wanted to enter an upcoming pageant. Not long after, a letter came from one of them. "I'm not very good in school," she wrote. "I don't participate in sports. I tried to play softball once, but I was awful. I danced for a year, and I was actually all right, at least that's what my teacher said, but I felt stupid. I was the only 14-year-old in the class, and everyone else was seven or eight. My last two boyfriends broke up with me because they didn't want their friends thinking that they were going out with such an ugly girl. But now I have filled out forms to enter the Miss Teen USA pageant because you and my mother are the only ones in my life who ever told me I was pretty. When my mom said I was pretty, it was kind of like she had to say it because she's my mom. But I think it's nice to hear someone else say it. That's why I wrote to you, to thank you."

Not only is teenagers' self-esteem affected by their own appearance; it is also affected by the appearance of family members, friends, and their belongings. Our friend Jack Marshall laughs about the time when he drove his children to high school, and they asked to be dropped off three blocks away from the building because they didn't want their friends to see Jack's old, beat-up Volkswagen bus.

WHICH MATTERS MOST?

Of these eight sources of self-esteem, which matters the most? Is it appearance or physical well-being? Is it performance or social acceptance? What is the source of self-esteem in teenagers with whom you work closely? It is difficult to pinpoint just one source because teens usually draw from a combination of these sources along with others unique to them individually. However, these sources offer a basic framework on which we can build.

"I wish cameras had never been invented. I hate pictures," one young woman said. However, the pictures that cause her frustration are not the ones taken with cameras. Rather, they are the ones she has developed in her own mind. Unfortunately, right now her self-esteem pictures are out of focus, fuzzy, and cloudy. Heavenly Father would rather have us focus on the positive. Each of us, teenagers and adults, must see clear pictures of ourselves—our true beauty, greatness, and eternal potential.

As parents and leaders, we need to be aware of the needs of the teenagers around us and do everything we can to help them see themselves as they really are, each one a child of God.

Keys to Action

Watch for the following types of responses, which are indicative of low self-esteem.

1. *Social acceptance: "I'm sure they're always talking about me behind my back."*
2. *Performance: "I'll make everyone happy only if I win the trophy."*
3. *Showing feeling: "I could never let him know how mad I am."*
4. *Opening up: "I'll never tell him what I'm really thinking."*
5. *Real versus ideal: "I wish I could look more like the stars in the movies."*
6. *Physical well-being: "I can't go to bed tonight because I have a huge test in the morning" or "No thanks, I'll just grab a candy bar."*
7. *Self-comparison: "If only my grades were as good as John's."*
8. *Appearance: "Oh no, another pimple" or "I just hate my hair.*

CHAPTER 2

It Spells PARENTS

As parents and leaders, we have a direct and powerful influence on how young people see themselves. How can we help them if they suffer from low self-esteem? What are some specific things we can do to help them feel better about themselves?

"My parents think, like, I'm a totally bad kid. But I don't think I am that bad. There are kids who are a lot worse than me. I don't go out drinking and stuff. They are always getting mad about little things that don't matter all that much."

How can adults help when they know a young person is suffering from low self-esteem? Here are some suggestions that can be remembered by thinking about the letters of the word P-A-R-E-N-T-S.

P stands for Praise.

A young man wrote, "My parents support me 100 percent. They are always there for me. As we grew up, my brothers and I participated in sports. My mother was at every one of our games. Mom and Dad are always there cheering us on and telling us how great we are when we get down."

Another young man wrote, "I wish my parents would praise me more. I hear, 'You can do better' a lot more than I hear 'That's really good.' I hear a lot more negatives than positives, and I think it should be the other way around."

In their book *Counseling, a Guide to Helping Others,* authors Terrance D. Olson and R. Lanier Britsch have written, "One reason children feel inadequate is that their adequacy has never been acknowledged by the adults in their lives."

Praise feeds the spirit just as food feeds the body. You know how much food teenagers' growing bodies can take in. How much food are we offering their growing spirits? According to a national PTA study on self-esteem, "Parents generous with kind words help their children keep a guard up against narcotics addiction and teenage pregnancy."

Barbara's daughter, by her own admission, was not a very good student in high school. Nevertheless, she had enthusiasm that wouldn't quit. Barbara and her husband kept their attention and comments directed to their daughter's strong points, telling her, "You are the sunshine of our home."

One mother found that in complimenting her daughter, it helped not only to be specific but also to look for distinctive and creative ways to express her feelings. For instance, once she left a note and candy bar on her daughter's bed. Another time she took out a personal ad in the local paper that read: "To Jessica—You brighten my day. Love, Mom."

One form of praise we have found to be effective is to find positive nicknames for the young people we work with. A boy named Dan might become "Dan the man." Ben might be called "Big Ben." Ray becomes "The King" and Linda is "Pretty" because that is what the words *Ray* and *Linda* mean in Spanish. Brad calls teenagers his Helaman's Warriors. In some cases, positive nicknames can be a sign of acceptance and make young people feel approved of and important. One boy said, "One thing my dad does that really helps me is finding uplifting nicknames for me. Like when I play football, he calls me Mr. Touchdown."

Some people believe that liberal amounts of praise make a teenager feel arrogant and conceited. On the contrary, it builds confidence and security. There are enough influences outside the Church and home that point out faults. Young people don't need parents and leaders to "keep them humble."

One bishop, after complimenting one of his struggling young women during a youth fireside, received what he thought to be a verbal slap in the face. He had said, "You look nice tonight." The girl responded, "No I don't. You're only saying that because you're the bishop."

When he later told us of this experience, we reminded him that young people who do not feel good about themselves usually do not know how to receive compliments well. We encouraged him to see through built-up defenses and remember that when people are starving, sometimes they reject the food they so badly need. We also suggested that in the future, the bishop try complimenting this particular girl in a private interview or with a telephone call. With teenagers, public praise is sometimes rejected because of the potential negative social stigma attached to being recognized before a group. One young man put it this way, "I'm proud of getting straight A's in school, but I don't want anyone to announce my grades over the loudspeaker because then the other guys start calling me 'the brain.'"

Our friend Randy Bird told about a young man in his seminary class who, when Brother Bird asked for reports from the youth on how much they had read in the scriptures, would reply that he hadn't read beyond First Nephi in the Book of Mormon. At the end of the school year, he told Brother Bird in private, "I just thought you'd like to know that I've finished the Book of Mormon."

"Why didn't you tell me sooner?" Brother Bird asked.

The young man, who was a state-champion wrestler and very popular with his peers, responded, "I didn't want people to think I was spiritual."

Before Barbara's daughter served her mission, she attended cosmetology school. She did exceptionally well, even taking first place in a state hair-design competition. That day she called Barbara excitedly and said, "Mom, guess what?" After sharing her good news, she added, "I knew you'd be happy to hear this." She called long distance because she knew that her mother would want to hear about her success and that she would praise her. She was right.

Negative comments seem to come so easily: "You move like a turtle." "How many times must I tell you that you just don't look good in that outfit?" Sometimes we pretend we are joking by quickly adding "just kidding" after a clever low cut. Ralph Waldo Emerson said, "Words are as hard as cannon balls." Young people feel those cannon balls when we casually or thoughtlessly say, "You're so stupid. You really give me gray hairs," or "I just can never count on you. I knew I'd end up doing your work." We must be careful. It is human nature for people to respond to what is said to and about them.

In a study of teachers conducted by the magazine *Childhood Education,* 25 percent said they *never* praised their students. Of the 75 percent who did praise students, half offered only bland, unenthusiastic acceptance with such comments as "OK" or "uh-huh." On the other hand, think of how often and consistently the scriptures record that Heavenly Father praised Jesus, saying, "This is my beloved son, in whom I am well pleased."

Mother Teresa has said, "Kind words can be short and easy to speak, but their echoes are truly endless." Brad's wife, Debi, has never forgotten an occasion in her teenage years when someone told her that in a meeting a leader had praised her for her dependability. While the leader didn't say the words directly to Debi, she learned about them, and they made a real difference in her self-esteem.

A young man named Matthew from O'Fallon, Illinois, told us, "I love it when parents and leaders praise me for the things I have accomplished, big or small. Some people think you outgrow the need for that, but I don't think anyone ever outgrows the need to be praised."

A stands for Accept.

A young woman wrote, "I wish my parents could more readily accept who I am instead of who they want me to be. They should encourage me in the activities I enjoy instead of always demanding that I do the things they want."

Teen years are a wonderful testing time. This is obvious in everything from the music and dress to the types of extracurricular activities young people select. As long as Church standards are not compromised, parents and leaders can accept choices teenagers make. We need to let them express their opinions and feelings freely.

One mother said, "My husband and I were not very happy when our son decided to get so heavily involved in sports in high school. We know that, in the long run, he would be better off putting his efforts toward getting better grades and preparing for college. But we listened to his point of view and accepted his decision."

Young people must never feel that adults accept them only when they do things our way. They must feel they are accepted for who they are. Young people are always individuals of great worth regardless of whether or not we think their present choices and actions are worthwhile.

When Barbara and her husband, Hal, got married, he said to her, "There's 80 percent of me that's good and 20 percent that's not so good. If you choose to dwell on my 80 percent, we're going to be happy." The same is true of teenagers. We need to dwell on their good qualities and help them to feel that we truly accept them for who they are.

A young man said, "My parents are always picking at me about something. It's like they want me to be perfect—and they want it right now." A 16-year-old Korean American youth said that everyone has the idea that "all Asians are smart. Having a reputation for brains is nice, I guess," he said, "but it can also be a pain. My father and mother expect an awful lot out of me. They want me to be number one." Another young woman wrote to Brad, "I am the oldest of many children. My father is the bishop, and I'm expected to be the perfect example for my brothers and sisters and the perfect Mormon for the ward. Sometimes my parents expect too much. I have to excel in everything I do and never be mediocre."

God has told us that he expects us to work toward becoming perfect, but true perfection does not come in this mortal life. He gives us several different estates in which to grow and progress toward that lofty goal, a pattern that we need to follow with our own children. Sometimes we hear the counsel, "Don't be mediocre." However, we should also remember that the word *mediocre* comes from the Latin word *medioais,* which means "halfway up the mountain." Mediocrity is not bad so long as it is not the final goal. Mediocrity is simply a halfway point through which everyone must pass on the way up the mountain. We all have to be mediocre before we can be anything beyond that.

Maybe a teenager isn't winning any contests. Maybe he or she isn't getting top grades. Maybe he or she is "mediocre." Well, what's so wrong with that? We're talking about teenagers. Right now is the time when they are supposed to be going through mediocrity in many areas. Perhaps a young man wants to be in debate, but his father wants him to be a track star. Maybe another young man is interested in car engines while his mother would rather have him developing his skills with people. Teenagers need to have opportunities to develop their own interests and talents. And having a messy room today doesn't mean a teenager's home will be messy at some future day. Wearing wrinkled clothes today doesn't mean a teenager will dress inappropriately for his or her first job interview.

One young man put it this way: "I wish my parents understood that my effort doesn't always correlate with my achievement. Sometimes I put forth a lot of effort and don't always have great achievement. But that achievement, however small, is a success for me because I have tried my best. I don't mind high expectations being put on me—like the standards in *For the Strength of Youth*—because that keeps me striving. But when expectations are too high or unrealistic, it is discouraging."

Prophets have stated the expectation that all worthy young men should serve missions. Such an expectation is healthy, unlike the expectation of a father who might say, "I hope you get called to Japan on your mission because they always send the smart ones to Japan, and then you'll have a good language for business school."

Imagine the son of this man receiving a call to serve in a neighboring state. Measured against the reasonable and selfless expectation of the prophet and the Lord, this young man's self-esteem can soar. Measured against the father's unreasonable and selfish expectation, his self-esteem will be challenged.

R stands for Respect.

"I wish my parents understood that the things I do are just because I'm an individual," a teenager said. "I wish they understood that I am me and my little brother is separated from me. We're two different people."

Barbara has coached five young women who have won the title of Miss USA. It surprises some to find out that Barbara's coaching does not involve teaching young women how to fit into the mold of a beauty queen. Rather, she helps each of them to discover and accentuate the things that are unique to them. That's what makes them winners.

One of these young ladies is Michelle Royer, who was named Miss Texas. As she was getting ready to go to the national Miss USA pageant, where she ultimately won the crown, she wrote to Barbara:

"I never could really put into words how much I appreciate you or how much I've grown in the past few months. When people ask me how you've helped me, I tell them that besides giving me Texas on a silver platter, you've given me the opportunity to learn on my own. Never before have I been able to rely so much on myself. That's a pretty good feeling, considering the next month ahead of me. It sure feels good not to be scared any more. Some of my so-called friends in school and in other beauty pageants make me, or should I say I let them make me, feel insecure because I never fit into their mold. You taught me there is no mold for Michelle Royer. I'm the only one, thank goodness. I hope that you'll be proud of me when I compete in the Miss USA pageant."

Barbara believes that one of the reasons Michelle won the pageant that year was because she figured out that she is a unique person. The people who met her and talked with her admired her confidence and relaxed manner. People respected her for her individuality.

Brad grew up in a family of all boys and no girls. His brothers all happened to be good athletes. Brad was not. He says, "My dad respected that. He expected me to learn how to handle a ball. He taught me how to catch, throw, dribble, and pass. But beyond that, he respected what I wanted to do." Brad attended his brothers' games and athletic events. They, in turn, attended his school plays and music recitals. Brad says, "I got negative put-downs at school for not being a very good ballplayer, and I always felt uncomfortable at Mutual, when every week the activity was the same: basketball. The thing that got me through all of that was being able to come home to a safe place where parents and family respected me for just being me."

Barbara says, "My mother once compared my sister, Paula, to me. She said something like, 'Well, you aren't getting the grades that Barbara got.' My sister really hated it when my mother said that. Such comparisons accomplish nothing. They do not motivate the child being talked to, and they do not reinforce or uplift the child being talked about. It's a losing situation in every respect."

E stands for Encourage.

A teenager offered some good advice for all parents: "Parents could compliment us on the little things and boost our egos up and encourage us. They could say, 'You can do whatever it is you want to do. We believe in you. It doesn't matter if you win. Just have fun!'"

When Sharlene Wells Hawkes competed in the Miss America pageant, she had some pretty discouraging times. Since the competitors usually stand in alphabetical order, as Miss Utah she was always standing next to Miss Texas, who had furs and diamonds. (As Miss Utah, Sharlene had won a simple, inexpensive wardrobe from a chain department store.) Many times, photographers would say, "Please move over, Miss Utah, so we can take a few pictures of Miss Texas." Sharlene would back out of the way. It was embarrassing.

On the night of the parade on the famous boardwalk at Atlantic City, New Jersey, where the pageant was held, each contestant had an opportunity to sit in a convertible and wave to the crowd while photographers took her picture and reporters interviewed her. When Miss Texas sat in the car, many flashes from the cameras went off and interviewers asked lots of questions. When it was Sharlene's turn, she sat in the convertible in her department-store dress and raised her hand to wave—but there was not one flash, not one question.

Sharlene walked back to the hotel and felt like crying. Then she bit her lip and told herself, "Oh no you don't, Sharlene. You have three things that you can count on. One is your belief in Jesus Christ. The second is your belief in yourself. The third is the fact that your family is behind you."

Her parents, Elder Robert E. Wells of the Quorum of the

Seventy and Sister Wells, had taught her to believe in Christ, in herself, and in her family. Their support and encouragement was consistent and unwavering. Had Sharlene not won the title of Miss America, she still would have come away from that pageant secure in the support of her family. She was a winner either way, and because she won the pageant, she became a winner *both* ways.

Sometimes even our smallest attempts to encourage teenagers can go a long way. Barbara received a letter from a young woman who told her, "I first met you at a youth conference. You came up to me and told me I was beautiful, which was the total opposite of what I believed at that time. Your comment caused me to reevaluate my self-image and make a turn around for the better. Now, I am married in the temple to a wonderful priesthood holder. One of my biggest goals is to encourage the youth and help them with self-esteem the way you helped me."

Chris, a 17-year-old from Huntington Beach, California, said, "I really love my parents. They support and encourage me in everything I do, and that is what probably helps me the most. When I feel that encouragement, it makes me feel that I don't have to go out and drink or party. It gives me self-confidence so I can overcome temptation. I don't think I'd be the kind of person I am without the encouragement and support of my parents."

N stands for Notice.

"Instead of always asking me to do more around the house, I wish my parents would thank me for what I've done and maybe notice that I'm trying to help," a teenager wrote.

One father said, "When my children became teenagers, I realized quickly that I needed to have eyes in the back of my head. Now I guess I need to train those eyes to see the positive and ignore the negative." Elder Vaughn J. Featherstone has said, "It's too easy sometimes to look at the dirt on the flower's petal rather than the beauty of the flower."

A friend of Brad's told him about a little experiment she tried with her teenage son. Rather than continuing to nag him as she had done for months for having a negative attitude around the house, she decided to simply compliment him when he did better. When he took out the garbage, she said, "Thank you." When his report card came home with mostly A's and B's but one D, she forced herself to say, "That's great that you have so many high grades" instead of jumping on him about the low grade that first caught her eye. At the end of several weeks she reported, "He is doing much better and his countenance has brightened around the house. All this time I kept thinking that my job was to change him and his attitude, but it was I who needed to change." She smiles when she adds, "I am finally learning to catch him doing something right instead of doing something wrong."

Along with noticing the good things teenagers do, it is also important to notice when they need to talk or open up. One girl told us, "My dad may not always be the most sensitive person in the world, but when something is really bothering me, he always seems to notice. He'll come up to my room and say, 'Want to talk about it?' I always say, 'How did you know something was wrong?' and he just smiles."

T stands for Time.

Studies have indicated that on an average, parents spend less than ten minutes a day talking with each of their children. And much of that talking is harsh, judgmental, and critical. No wonder Elder Jeffrey R. Holland of the Seventy said that we must "spend more of our time with and devote more of our energy to the good things, the best things, the things that endure and bless and pre-vail." We love the Church's radio advertisement that says, "So you want to build a relationship with your teenager? Take your time."

Many families find that the only way to bring busy lives together is to make time rather than wait for time. One father said, "I look at it this way. If I were invited to attend a dinner at the White House or to do something else I really wanted to do, that strong desire would alter my schedule. I would simply make time for it. It is said that good intentions will never replace good atten-tions."

Family home evening is a wonderful opportunity for time together. Teenagers may say they don't like it, but they do. Brad tells about when his daughter Wendee was in second grade and he asked what her favorite part of school was.

She said, "Recess."

Brad asked, "What do you do at recess?"

"Chase the boys."

"What do you do when you catch the boys?"

"We take them to jail."

"What do you do with them when they are in jail?"

"We hug 'em."

Brad said, "Wendee, you'd better stop that. The boys don't like it."

She said, "Daddy, they say they don't like it, but they do."

Even though teens may resist at first, they really do like it when parents and leaders spend time with them. Time together can reduce the influences of the outside world and increase the influ-ences we have on each other.

Try surprising teenagers with a picnic at a park or "kidnapping" them and taking them to a show. Once Barbara's mother picked up her and her best friend for a surprise lunch during the school day. When Barbara's two children were growing up, she would occasionally give them a special day when they got to go anywhere they wanted to go with her. Her daughter once wanted to go to the beauty parlor and get a manicure. They did it. Her son wanted to go a popular shopping center to have ice cream and chocolate chip cookies for breakfast. They did it.

Both Brad and his wife, Debi, spent several years overseas with their families as they were growing up. They both look back at those times as wonderful, bonding experiences. Debi says, "The reason it was great was not just because we were involved with another culture, but because we were together with our families more. We became very close to our families and learned to depend on them. That time together made a difference."

S stands for Say.

"The thing I have the hardest time with is that my parents still treat me like I'm a baby," one teenager lamented. "The leaders at the Church do too. It's as if I can't be trusted to do anything on my own, and what I think or want to do makes no difference even if I have a good idea."

Unrealistic expectations, habitual nagging, or long lists of "musts," "don'ts," and "can'ts" often leave young people feeling helplessly fenced in. As parents and leaders, we need to give them a say in the things that affect them and their lives. They must be able to express their opinions, give input, make changes, and affect their environment. We must offer them a voice in deciding on the nature and complexity of their goals.

One father of eight children said, "Kids need guidelines, and when I have to say no, I'm not afraid to say it. In my job I have guidelines, and people say no to me a lot. But within those guidelines, I also have freedom in my work, a sense of ownership that makes what I do fulfilling and satisfying. That's the same kind of balance and ownership I try to offer my teenagers."

The year before Brad went on his mission, he had the opportunity to serve as the only youth representative on the national executive board of the Boy Scouts of America. He worked with remarkable men—presidents of large companies and corporations—who were making important decisions about the future of the scouting program.

At one meeting, the board members discussed why Scouts refused to wear the pants of the Scout uniform. After a long and loud discussion about cost of the pants and whether they were comfortable, the chairman turned to Brad and said, "You're our youth representative. Tell us, why won't the Scouts wear the pants?" Everyone in the room turned and looked expectantly at the 18-year-old member of their board.

Brad cleared his throat, took a deep breath, and said, "It has nothing to do with comfort or cost, it's just that the pants look really geeky. They're not cool." Lightbulbs went on. Heads nodded. Assignments were made. The board members were glad a young person had been given a chance to express his views. Brad still smiles when he sees the new uniforms—more fashionable, more athletic looking, and definitely more "cool."

P-A-R-E-N-T-S. As easily as we can spell the word, we can remember to build self-esteem in teenagers by Praising, Accepting, Respecting, Encouraging, Noticing, spending Time with them, and giving them a Say in their lives. Each of these suggestions may have to be tailored to fit individual circumstances, for just as each child is unique, so each will react differently. But as we seek the guidance of the Spirit, we can find unique ways to tailor our actions and responses so that the self-esteem of those teenagers for whom we are responsible will improve.

Keys to Action

To build teenagers' self-esteem, put into practice the seven ideas suggested by the word PARENTS:

1. **Praise.** Comment on their strongest points, such as "You're the sunshine in our home." Find and use positive nicknames, such as "Big Ben," "Mr. Touchdown," "Princess," "Miss Gorgeous."

2. **Accept.** Try to accept the choices they make, such as in sports, school subjects, or special interests. And don't expect perfection: remember that there is good in everyone just as there are some things that may be not so good. Look for the good!

3. **Respect.** Allow them to develop their own individuality. Respect their uniqueness and help them to feel that "it's okay to be me."

4. **Encourage.** Let them know you are behind them 100 percent so that they have the courage to press forward. Give them your support and try to build their confidence.

5. **Notice.** Pay attention to and talk about their accomplishments. Don't always be critical, observing only their faults and weaknesses. Notice when their moods change or when they may need to talk.

6. **Time.** Make time rather than wait for a time to be together. They may say they don't like to do things together as a family, but they really do.

7. **Say.** Let them to have a say in the things that affect their lives. Give them guidelines, but allow them to make some of their own choices and decisions.

CHAPTER 3

The Importance of Self-worth

Knowledge of true self-worth can give young people a solid view of their great value. What is self-worth? What is the difference between self-esteem and self-worth? How can we really help teenagers discover who they truly are and how much they are actually worth?

"When I feel depressed, it always helps me to sing Church songs. I sing 'I Am a Child of God' and 'I Am of Infinite Worth' and 'I Feel My Savior's Love.' The lyrics of those songs lift my heart because they remind me of who I really am and how valuable I am to Heavenly Father and Jesus. My Young Women president told something once that has always stayed with me. She said, 'We didn't come to earth to find self-worth—we brought it with us.'"

T hey're just beautiful!" the wife exclaimed as she opened the gift from her husband and excitedly took out diamond earrings to match her wedding band. "Thank you," she said sincerely.

Her husband beamed to see his wife so pleased. She had once mentioned that someday she would like such a pair of earrings. He had saved a little each month for several years in order to buy them. The only problem was that his wife, thinking that there was no way in the world the husband could have afforded real diamonds, thought they were cubic zirconias.

In the months that followed, she wore the earrings casually.

She was careless when she put them on and took them off, and finally she misplaced one. When she told her husband, he became very concerned. Only then did she realize that the diamonds were real. The worth of the stones had never changed. What *had* changed was how she esteemed the stones.

In the same way, it is essential for young people to realize that regardless of how they presently esteem themselves, they are of great worth. That fact never changes.

The many self-esteem seminars, movements, task forces, councils, musical presentations, and school training programs being offered today all miss the final mark if they do not lead participants past self-esteem to actual self-worth. Without this perspective, such self-esteem programs and efforts are, as one critic has said, shallow, hollow, and "the latest national elixir."

Why do young people lose self-esteem? There are both external and internal reasons. Externally, adults need to realize that self-esteem is not something we give someone so much as it is something we must stop taking away. Internally, young people must realize that their worth has never changed. Just as with the diamonds, as low as their self-esteem may plunge, their worth is still very great. Brigham Young taught, "The greatest lesson you can learn is to know yourselves." How can we help young people discover who they are?

True self-worth, like true religion, is revealed. An understanding of our true identities comes from the same source all truth comes from—God. Many in the world today, much like the churches and sects of Joseph Smith's day, exist on part truths, having the appearance of self-esteem but denying the power thereof. As surely as Joseph did, each of us needs a pillar of light—a clear picture of God, our relationship to him, and the knowledge that what we are doing is in accordance with his will for us. Esteem will increase as we discover our eternal worth.

One young woman Brad knows struggled with self-esteem during her teen years. She told him, "So-and-so told me I'm too fat, and so-and-so told me I'm not fun to be with. I'm not as pretty or popular as my best friend. Not one boy has ever asked me out."

Brad asked, "Did you ever go to the carnival fun house and look in the mirrors?"

"Yes," she said, "but what does that have to do with anything?"

Brad explained, "Those mirrors distort the truth. If we really believe the image of ourself that we see in those mirrors, it could cause some major problems. Can you imagine curling your hair or putting on makeup using one of those mirrors? It's the same way with self-esteem. Using the eyes of the world as our only mirrors will leave us with a distorted view. What others think of us or say about us is important, but it can't be our only source of information."

George D. Durrant has written, "What someone else thinks about me is not the driving force for me that it once was." That is the point that we must all reach: making self-esteem less horizontal (relying on the input and influence of others) and more vertical (relying on the input and influence of God).

After talks at youth conferences and education weeks, people often approach speakers and say something kind. Casual onlookers might wonder if this praise is the source of self-esteem for these speakers. What those onlookers do not see or hear are the jealous comments and hurtful letters that sometimes come, criticizing even the most sincere efforts of teachers who are in such a public arena. For those whose only source of self-esteem is the input of others, such comments could lead to their no longer speaking. However, most speakers in the Church do what they do in order to serve God and their brothers and sisters in the gospel. This knowledge brings balance. It doesn't matter how many people express compliments after a lecture if the teacher does not feel that God is pleased with his or her motives and work. On the other hand, some people may criticize a teacher and find fault, but if the teacher honestly feels that God is pleased with his or her offerings, he or she can be at peace. God validates worth regardless of how others esteem.

"The only sure anchor to personal security is in God and in God's definition of man," according to Stephen R. Covey. In the temple we learn much about God's definition of man. We are reminded of our literal kinship with him. We are all his spirit children and are of infinite worth. We wear white robes as a symbol of purity and to help eliminate any distinction between rich and poor. No hoods or tassels are worn by those with worldly degrees and titles. No tags or ribbons indicate a bishop or Relief Society president. In the temple we are all equal. The qualifications for entering the temple do not include beauty or talent or worldly acclaim. The only requirement for wearing temple robes is personal worthiness.

What can parents and leaders do to help young people feel closer to God and realize their individual worth? One excellent way is to involve them in service. A bishop on the BYU campus, Thomas E. Myers, said, "Young people with low self-esteem are in a downward cycle. Service is the cycle breaker. As they become busy serving and blessing and healing others, they will not even notice that they are being blessed and healed themselves." As we help to raise in teenagers a healthy concern for others, we diminish the effects of their unhealthy concern for self.

Patricia T. Holland said that when her husband, Jeffrey R. Holland, became president of BYU and their family moved to a new home on the campus, her teenage son, Matt, had a difficult and insecure time of adjustment. He prayed every night that he would make his high school's varsity basketball team, be a good student, and have enough confidence to make friends. Later, when he was serving his mission, Matt realized something important. He said, "I had gone about the confidence matter in entirely the wrong way. It was only in my intense and heartfelt desire to serve others as a missionary that I found what true confidence really was. When asking for my own needs [to be met] in those high school years, I was not reassured. Even now if I ask for his help to have more popularity or to look good in the eyes of others, I lose that confidence. But on my mission when I wanted to reach unbelievers for *their* sake, for what I knew I could give *them*, I had the confidence of Joshua and Jeremiah combined."

Brad had a difficult time in junior high school. A boy who has no basket-shooting skills often suffers in elementary school and agonizes in junior high. The students in junior high came from several different elementary schools, and many who suffered from insecurity picked on others.

Somehow, in the shuffle, Brad ended up at the bottom of the pecking order. Each day he had to face the threats, rejection, and hurtful criticisms of classmates. Once he was in that position, it seemed as if nothing he did was right. If he tried to talk and be friendly, he was mocked. If he didn't, others made fun of him anyway. He hated the pain and the hurt. But—and this is the point—through it all he did not hate himself.

Brad says, "I always had the feeling that they just didn't know me. Because of the praise, acceptance, and encouragement I'd received from parents and Church leaders, I liked myself. Because I knew I was valuable in God's eyes, I valued myself. The fact that the kids at school didn't like me did not seem like evidence that I was a bad person. Rather it was simply evidence that they did not know me."

As Brad and his classmates grew and matured, they came to know each other better. Brad reached out in service, and his efforts brought acceptance. In fact, when awards were passed out at his senior-class dinner dance in high school, Brad was not voted best-looking or most likely to succeed. Instead he was given an award that meant much more to him than any other award ever could. He was named the most-loved senior. This award came from many of the same students who literally spat on him in the halls of their junior high.

Brad's self-esteem was tested, but because of a knowledge of his true self-worth, he was able to weather the storm. Perhaps, in a small way, this is the same sense of strength that the Prophet Joseph Smith felt during his life. Once when he was being served a warrant after accusations against him had been dismissed in a trial, he wrote, "The constable who served this second warrant upon me had no sooner arrested me than he began to abuse and insult me; and so unfeeling was he with me, that although I had been kept all the day in court without anything to eat since the morning, yet he hurried me off to Broome county, a distance of about fifteen miles, before he allowed me any kind of food what-ever. He took me to a tavern, and gathered in a number of men who used every means to abuse, ridicule and insult me. They spit upon me, pointed their fingers at me, saying, 'Prophesy, prophesy!'

THE IMPORTANCE OF SELF-WORTH

and thus did they imitate those who crucified the Savior of mankind, not knowing what they did." *(History of the Church* 1:91.)

These wicked men did not know who the Prophet was. They did not esteem him. Though they were in the presence of a valuable diamond, they were treating him like mere glass. Nevertheless, Joseph knew exactly who he was. He knew his relationship to God, and he knew his worth in God's eyes. This knowledge allowed him to act accordingly and to weather the severest of storms.

The greatest thing we can do to help young people improve self-esteem is to help them come to know the Savior. Through coming to know him, they will come to know of their self-worth, and when they know their true worth, their self-esteem will be increased.

As Barbara concluded a class in a ward she was visiting, the bishop walked up to the front of the room and asked, "May I say something?" Barbara handed the microphone to him, and he told he following story:

When I was eight years old, I was really into baseball. I had every player's baseball card. My dad saved his money to send me to a baseball camp run by a star player.

The first day, the famous man running the camp—a man who was kind of cocky—pulled out a list of names and asked, "Where's Step-han?" My name is spelled S-t-e-p-h-e-n, which is pronounced like Steven. He purposely mispronounced it.

I cringed as everyone started to laugh.

The coach continued to call, "Step-han, are you here? Hey, Step-han."

I felt worse and worse. Everyone was laughing harder and harder. It was the worst experience of my life. When I got home, I told my dad I would never play baseball again.

My dad was a wise man and waited a few years. Then a retired player came to town and started a Little League program. Dad took the new coach aside and said, "My son loves baseball very much, but he had a bad experience with a coach." And he told the new coach the whole story.

The new coach said, "You send him to me for tryouts."

I barely made the team, but I improved as the season progressed. Then the time came when it was a win-or-lose situation for my team. The bases were loaded, and it was my turn at bat. I thought the coach was going to send in a pinch hitter for me, but he didn't. He walked over and put his arm around me and said, "Stephen, you can do it. I'm your coach, and I'm behind you all the way. You can do it."

I walked up to the plate, and the pitcher threw the ball. I did not hit it out of the ballpark, but I did hit a fly to the center fielder that was deep enough to allow the runner from third to beat the throw to home. Our team won the game.

I'll never forget that coach. Then I grew up and got another coach in my life. My new coach came to me one night and said, "Stephen, you're going on a mission." And when I said to him, "I don't think I can do it," he said, "Yes, you can. I have faith in you. I know you can do it." My new coach was Jesus Christ.

I went on a mission. Then my coach came to me again one night, after I had gotten married, and said, "Stephen, you're going to be in charge of the Blazer Bs." I said, "I can't be in charge of them." And my coach, the Savior, said, "Yes, you can. I have faith in you."

Two months ago he came to me again and said, "Stephen, you're going to be the bishop." I said, "I can't be the bishop." And the Savior said, "I'll be right beside you every step of the way."

This bishop had learned to listen to the one who knew the real Stephen and who knew his potential. His coach would support him.

The best way to help young people increase self-esteem is to help them recognize their self-worth. We must help them overlook the denigrating voices of the world and get a new coach—someone who knows them, loves them, and sees them for the true diamonds they are. We must help them to make the *Savior* their coach.

In her book *Lighten Up,* Chieko Okazaki provides an excellent summary for this chapter. "We hear a lot about self-esteem these days. Self-esteem—the kind that really counts—comes from a relationship with Jesus Christ and Heavenly Father that is real and solid and alive. Not a secondhand relationship of listening to someone else talk about them, but a firsthand relationship of talking with them, of experiencing their love, of being their hands in serving others."

Keys to Action

As caring parents and leaders, we can help teenagers to understand that self-esteem and self-worth are not the same thing. We can teach them that—

1. Self-esteem is belief in oneself but self-worth is our divine heritage, our true worth in the sight of God.
2. True self-worth, like true religion, is revealed. An understanding of our true identities comes from the same source as all truth: from God.
3. In order to know themselves, they must first come to know God and Christ.
4. They need to learn how to make self-esteem less horizontal (relying on the input and influence of others) and more vertical (relying on the input and influence of God).
5. One of the best ways to increase self-esteem and enhance self-worth is to become involved in service. As we help them raise a healthy concern for others, the effects of their negative feelings for self will diminish. In service they can find self-acceptance.

CHAPTER 4

Hear Them Cry

Teenagers often build walls that seem impenetrable—walls of protection against mistrust, insecurity, and fears. What are these walls and how do we recognize them? Once we are brought up against these walls, how can we work to break them down?

"I think there are things wrong with me. Deep inside there is someone crying for help, but I have built a wall and blocked out everyone who tries to help. I don't cry anymore—at least not on the outside."

I t's as though there's a wall there," one mother said. "When my daughter was younger it was easy. We talked regularly and openly. But as she got older, this wall went up." She shook her head. "Why won't she talk to me anymore?"

This mother is not alone in her frustration. Many parents and leaders know about walls teenagers sometimes build. They seem high and impenetrable. Some even appear to be covered with barbed wire and plastered with "Keep Out" signs. Yet, walls can come down. At this time in history, we are all witnesses that even the most seemingly permanent walls can come down.

Teenagers build walls for protection, or out of insecurity, distrust, fear, and misunderstanding. How can we most effectively address those concerns? How can we talk to teenagers who don't particularly want to talk to us? How can we make ourselves into the kind of people teenagers will open up to? How can we bring down those walls? Parents and leaders must first see beyond the wall and find the "loose brick."

SEE BEYOND THE WALL

"I think the best thing about my bishop is that he doesn't get scared off by teenagers even when we give him a hard time," a teenager told us. "He tells us how much he loves us—the youth, the terrible, awful, disrespectful rebels who defy all authority and are out to ruin the world. At least that's how some people see us just because we have different hairstyles and don't wear the same styles of clothes they wear. But my bishop sees though it all. He tells us he cares about us and that's all we really want to know— that someone out there cares."

Some teenagers wear extreme hairstyles, torn jeans, and T-shirts plastered with the names of rock groups. Some have tattoos and chains and use vulgar words and gestures. Others are well-groomed but cocky, rude, and defiant. Still others seem distant and unmotivated. In all of these cases, adults receive strong signals that seem to say "Leave me alone and stay out of my life." We must see beyond the facade.

A young person's emotions and needs are usually expressed in coded messages—secret codes, if you will—that we must receive and interpret. It's really nothing new. Remember when your child was a baby? He cried, and you didn't know why. You tried changing him. Still he cried. You tried feeding him, rocking him. You thought, "I can't figure this kid out! I wish he could just talk to me and tell me what he wants!"

Now that little one is a teenager and guess what? He is still playing the same game. He no longer needs a diaper change or bottle. He needs security, acceptance, attention, and positive reinforcement. But he doesn't voice those needs any more clearly now than when he was a baby. He just gives you the signals and expects you to figure out what he needs. In his own way, he is still crying. Only now, the tears are inside. Elder Marvin J. Ashton said, "I hear people crying to us when they don't even know they are crying."

One year for our class during Education Week, we prepared a slide presentation with a song that was written by our friend Kenneth Cope. The first pictures were of babies crying as Kenneth sang, "There's a cry in the night as another life begins. Tiny one pleads for love today." The next slides were of teenagers. Kenneth sang about how children grow and their cries turn inward. Our favorite line in the song is a question, "Can wounds concealed be recognized?" It is up to us to "Hear them cry the tears they hide. Love means time. Hear them cry." Not long after Education Week ended, we received the following letter from a mother:

"When I got home from Ed Week today, my 17-year-old daughter's belongings were packed. She was ready to move out. I felt a knot in my stomach and my heart ached. But I remembered what you said, 'Hear them cry.' I knelt and prayed to know what I should say and do. . . . I approached her but heard only negative comments. For the first time, instead of getting defensive and upset, I heard her crying on the inside. I realized how much pain she must be feeling to be acting like this. Then I said calmly, 'Let's go talk in my room.' She not only followed, she smiled. I shared my feelings with her and opened up. I expressed my love and hurt and sadness, and she did not back away. She didn't get angry. She didn't fight me. She shared with me! For the first time ever we shared and talked like friends and not enemies. Then we went back in her room and put her things away."

Do you love me? Do you care? Am I a priority in your life? Such questions rarely come directly from teenagers, but they do come. Often, the most important part of communication is to hear what *isn't* being said. Just as with a crying baby, we have to do a lot of guessing, testing, and putting ourselves in teenagers' shoes to begin to understand. What are they feeling from behind their walls? Are they feeling insecure, ugly, untalented, stupid, scared, lonely, rejected, frustrated, or vulnerable? Here are some of the clues, or the "walls" that let you know your teenager is crying:

1. Creating distance

As teenagers pull away from the family or group and appear to be vague, withdrawn, or evasive, it is often a silent cry. When they don't look us in the eyes when we are talking or they avoid us when we are coming in their direction, we know there are tears falling inside. Of course, the natural reaction is to also pull back and tell ourselves, "I know when I'm not wanted," or "If that's how she feels about me, then I won't push myself into her life," or "If she's not going to talk to me, then I won't talk to her." We must fight this natural tendency. We need to act rather than react toward our teenagers.

Duane E. Hiatt, who has reared ten sons and three daughters, described how he searched for answers when one of his teenage sons became distant: "The greatest revelation I got from all the reading I did was this simple but profound thought: Whether my son spoke to me or not didn't change the fact that I could speak to him. Even if it was just one-way communication, at least he'd know how I felt. And I felt that this would keep the channels open so that he would always know that I would be there if he needed me." Brother Hiatt approached his son and said, "I know a little bit about what you're going through. I just want you to know that I know you can do it, that I love you and have confidence in you."

Adolescents find it difficult to know how to act. Are they supposed to be big children or little adults? Moping around and pulling away is sometimes a teenager's way of mentally trying on new roles to see how they fit. When this happens, hear them cry.

2. Extreme behavior

Teenagers who tend to be either extremely quiet or extremely loud are trying to communicate something from behind the wall. "That kid is so cocky. He needs a good humbling," we might say when, in reality, he needs just the opposite, to be built up and validated. Put-on pride is nothing more than a strategy he is using because inside he is feeling small, passed-over, unimportant, or jealous.

Teenagers who are extremely judgmental and can't find one good thing to say about any other person are probably trying desperately to find one good thing they like about themselves. Hear them cry.

3. "I have a friend who . . . "

A professional counselor told one mother, "Suppose your son came home and said, 'I have a friend who is taking drugs.' What would you say to him?"

The mother paused for a moment and then replied, "I'd probably tell him to find another friend." Like many parents, this mother was in the habit of reacting and making judgments before she had a clue about what was really going on. Whenever a child tells you about "my friend's problem," there is a good chance that child is struggling with a similar one. Young people drop hints about "friends" to test our reactions. If we are hasty, harsh, and judgmental, they may not want to open up any further. Hold off on judgments long enough to hear them cry.

4. Giving nonverbal signals

Some convincing research points out that the average person hears only about 7 percent of what is said with words. Another 55 percent of what is communicated comes from body language, and 38 percent comes from the tone of voice. Thus, it is important for parents and leaders to learn to listen with their eyes and hearts as well as with their ears. In short, we must be aware that teenagers' true attitudes and feelings are usually expressed through gestures, posture, rate of speech, voice tone, volume, and eye placement.

We need to notice the expressions on their faces, the look in their eyes, the way they hold their heads. We can detect boredom, hostility, or fatigue simply by observing the fidgeting of their legs and the movement of their hands. Watch carefully for nonverbal signals. Hear them cry.

5. Trying to attract attention

People who teach children know that overtly negative behavior is often just a ploy to attract attention. The same thing is true of teenagers. Childish pranks like giggling in class and pulling hair give way to swearing, wearing black clothes, wearing a single earring, using weird symbols, and sporting outlandish hairstyles. All such negative behavior is sending the same message: "Pay attention to me. Please notice me as an individual and appreciate the fact that I am different."

When teenagers make rash statements such as "I hate school," "My teacher is an idiot," "The Church isn't true," or "There is no

God," they are often just wanting someone to notice that they are frustrated. We must be careful not to take at face value the "wrong" things young people do or say. In such situations, young people may not feel as unsure about the truth as they feel unsure about themselves. Hear them cry.

6. Inconsistent behavior

Any noticeable difference between usual behavior and current behavior is often a cry for help. One girl who consistently did well in school suddenly started missing the bus. It drove her mother crazy. The girl would say, "I'm coming," but then she'd dawdle around in the mornings until she missed the bus and her mother had to take her to school.

The mother tried to reason with her daughter, telling her, "This is ridiculous. You're a mature, responsible person. You shouldn't need to be babied along in the morning." The girl agreed and caught the bus the next few days. Then she began missing it again. The mother said, "This is not like you. I have always been able to count on you. If you miss the bus again, I'll take you, but you'll have to pay me."

The following morning, the mother ended up having to drive the girl to school. When they arrived, she said, "That will be three dollars and a thank-you."

The girl blew up. "Taxi drivers don't get thanked!" she said indignantly.

The mother drove away from the school with her daughter still in the car. At last she had heard her daughter's cries. The mother said, "We need to talk." It seems the girl was having a hard time in her first-period class. She was not understanding the teacher and was feeling stupid. There were also some boys in that class who were teasing her about her high moral standards. Now mother and daughter were finally addressing the real problems, which had very little to do with catching a school bus. When teenagers' behavior is inconsistent, hear them cry.

FIND THE "LOOSE BRICK"

After hearing them cry, we must then find the "loose brick."

"The thing my mom does that I love is that she likes what I like even though she's old," a teenager explained. "She doesn't think that what I like is stupid or just some passing fad. She doesn't say my tastes are immature."

Our friend Rand Packer taught us a valuable principle about breaking down walls when he stated, "Having laid a few brick walls in my time, I have discovered that every wall has a weakness, a brick that is loose."

When we work with young people who have built walls around themselves, we must find the loose brick—the one interest, dream, or ability that is each person's favorite thing. It may be motorcycles, sports, food, the opposite sex, or even a journal.

One young man from New York who attended a youth program at Brigham Young University stayed to himself at first. His youth counselor was concerned and told the program director, "He just stays in his room and writes in his journal." Was this the loose brick the director needed?

That evening at dinner, the director purposely sat by the young man in the cafeteria. He began a normal conversation and then changed the subject to journals. The director said, "People don't usually believe me when I say it, but one of my favorite things to do is to write in my journal. I've already filled several volumes."

"Really?" The boy's eyes lit. "I write in my journal too. I think it's important." That was a turning point. The young man began to come to activities and to interact with others. Before the program ended, he had made many new friends. It all started when someone showed a little interest in his big interest.

We have found that loose bricks come in all varieties, shapes, and sizes: violas, guitars, soccer balls, oil paints, baby sisters, computers, and horses are some we have encountered recently.

Elder Vaughn J. Featherstone, in his book *A Generation of Excellence,* told of trying to reach a struggling young man in his Sunday School class. The boy never spoke to him, but Elder Featherstone found out that he had tried out for the sophomore football team. Imagine the boy's surprise when his Sunday School teacher showed up at his practice. "What are you doing here?" the boy asked.

"I came to watch you practice."

"Oh, you didn't come to watch me. What else are you here for?"

"I *did* come to watch you. I don't know any other guy on the team."

The boy went into the huddle, and several times during the next few minutes he looked over to see if his Sunday School teacher was still there.

President Lorenzo Snow once counseled a group of departing missionaries, "There is a way to reach every human heart, and it is your business to find the way to the hearts of those to whom you are called [to serve]."

After a class we taught during BYU's Education Week, a mother approached us and said, "But there is no way to reach my daughter. She simply does not have any loose bricks—a few loose screws maybe, but no loose bricks."

"Sure she does," we assured her. "What does she talk about or bring up in conversation?"

"Nothing."

"What does she do in her free time if she has her own choice?"

"Nothing. She just goes to school and work."

"Then what does she do with the money she earns?"

"She buys lots of clothes," the mother answered.

We smiled at her. "Guess what you just found?"

Three questions: What does the teenager talk most about? What does the teenager do or want to do with his or her free time? Where does your teenager put his or her own money? Answers to these can help us locate that loose brick. Then it is just a matter of spending the time required to push and pull at it until we break through the wall.

Barbara learned how important it is to see beyond the wall and find the loose brick when her daughter was 15 years old. That summer her daughter attended a state-run camp in California to which she had looked forward all year. But after she came home, Barbara noticed a big change in her. She was more distant from the family. Her moods were extreme. She wasn't taking care of her appearance, which was inconsistent for her.

At the time, Barbara did not recognize the cries she was hearing. She didn't think of approaching her daughter to talk. Problems continued, and finally Barbara made it a matter of prayer. She asked Heavenly Father to help her know what was wrong with her daughter.

One evening, her daughter went babysitting and left her journal open by the front door. That was not like her at all. Barbara picked it up and began to read. The more she read, the more horrified she became. A camp counselor with whom her daughter had been corresponding appeared to be a lesbian. Barbara says, "I cannot tell you what I felt at that time. I took the journal and showed my husband. He was irate that this camp counselor had been allowed to work with young girls at the camp. He wanted the people responsible to realize what was happening."

In the meantime, Barbara didn't know what to do about her daughter. She met with her three dearest LDS friends. They all advised her to seek help from her priesthood leaders, and the priesthood leaders in turn suggested that she seek professional help as well. Barbara went to three different psychologists until she found the one who gave her the advice that really helped her.

The counselor told Barbara that she had to talk with her daughter openly about the whole thing. Nothing could have been more frightening for Barbara. It seemed much easier to just keep going through her mothering motions as if nothing were wrong. The counselor told her that she had to be honest with her daughter and tell her she had read her journal.

The next day, Barbara sat down with her daughter and told her everything. Her daughter was absolutely devastated that Barbara had read her journal. She said, "Mom, are you calling me a—"

Barbara interrupted her and said, "No, I'm not calling you anything. I'm just saying that the friend you are writing to seems to be on the wrong track. She is much older than you, and I feel very strongly that you shouldn't be a friend with her anymore." Her daughter ran out of the room in tears. Easy experience? No. Fun? No. Necessary? Yes. Did Barbara handle it the way she should? She didn't know. She was simply doing the best she knew how to do at the time.

In the days that followed, the counselor advised Barbara to spend more time bonding with her daughter. Barbara had raised her daughter the same way she had raised her son, and now she realized that certain children need more love and attention. She thought that perhaps because she didn't give her daughter all the love she needed, she was being enticed outside the home by another kind of love. The counselor told Barbara to try to communicate, to let her daughter talk, and then to listen to her.

Barbara didn't know where to begin. She did not think about loose bricks at the time. She felt overwhelmed by the task ahead of her. "My teenage daughter hated me so much," she says. "I can still feel the horrible feeling in the pit of my stomach when I think about it. It is such a hopeless feeling when your own child hates you."

Barbara knew her daughter didn't care to be with her right then, but Barbara also knew that her daughter was 15 and cared a lot about being in a car. Barbara told her, "Okay, you want to learn to drive a car, right? I guess I'll just have to pick you up after school every day so you can practice."

Each afternoon Barbara would pick up her daughter, who would climb into the car, slam the door, and not say a word. Barbara would let her practice driving a while and then she would say, "I haven't eaten anything since breakfast. Would you mind if we stop at the bakery for a bagel?"

Day after day they would sit in the bakery, eating their bagels. Barbara says, "And for the first time in my life I shut up." Eventually her daughter started talking. She would tell her mother about her day. Then she started telling Barbara about the things that were going on in her life. It took almost the entire year, but things did start to get better. Barbara had to give up some control in exchange for some trust, but it was worth it.

It is important to note here, however, that the bottom-line

answer to this story was more than simply that Barbara gave up some control in exchange for some trust. Although this did take place, the real answers to stories such as this one come from Heavenly Father. This particular problem happened to be one of the most difficult challenges Barbara ever faced in her life. She fasted every Sunday for six months, and fasting is a sacrifice for Barbara because she gets migraines. The point of this isn't to highlight the sacrifices Barbara made, but to convey that the true answers lie in turning to our Heavenly Father. Although professional counselors can help, the counselor who helped the most was Heavenly Father.

That summer, Barbara took her daughter on every one of the youth conference assignments she was scheduled to do. She told her she needed someone to sing in her workshops. Her daughter, who has a beautiful voice, went with Barbara and sang.

Years passed. Barbara's daughter went on to graduate from high school and was preparing to go to Utah for school. The two of them sat on the floor of the bedroom and packed. Barbara's daughter came across her old journals. She opened one and read to her mother all the things she had been going through during that dark time in her life. She confessed that she had even considered committing suicide. Now she looked at her mother and said, "Mom, I'm so glad I didn't do that. I'm so glad we became best friends."

Recently at a parenting workshop at BYU, Barbara felt prompted to share this very personal story. She didn't know her daughter was in the back of the room listening (her daughter by this time had served a mission and had married in the temple). At the end of the talk, her daughter came to the front of the room and asked permission to sing a song. She then sang "Be That Friend."

As the introduction of the song began, Barbara's daughter said, "I want you all to know that my mom really is my best friend."

"Please learn from my mistakes," Barbara says. "Hear the cries of your teenagers early. Find the loose brick—the one thing your child wants to do or to talk about enough that he or she will even put up with having you there. Then really listen, communicate, and be that friend.

Keys to Action

Young people build walls for protection or because of insecurity, distrust, fear, and misunderstanding. Here are some suggestions of ways to penetrate those walls and help them.

First, see beyond the wall. Hear their silent cries. Listen to what isn't being said. Just as with a crying baby, we have to do a lot of guessing, testing, and putting ourselves in their shoes before we begin to understand. Watch for these clues to let you know they are crying:

1. **Creating distance,** such as pulling away from the family group, withdrawing, being evasive, or avoiding looking you in the eye.
2. **Extreme behavior,** such as unconventional, radical, or drastic changes in internal or external behavior.
3. **"I have a friend who . . . "**—a phrase that may be a signal they are talking about themselves.
4. **Nonverbal** signals, an indication of true feelings expressed through gestures, posture, rate of speech, voice tone and volume, and eye placement.
5. **Trying to attract attention,** behavior that says "Pay attention to me—notice me as an individual."
6. **Inconsistent behavior,** acting in a way that is noticeably different than the person's usual behavior.

Second, find the loose brick. When we work with young people who have built walls around themselves, we must find the loose brick—the one interest, dream, or ability that is each person's favorite thing.

CHAPTER 5

And the Walls Come Tumbling Down

What can we do to ensure that the walls teenagers have built will come down? How do we maintain open communication to prevent them from building new walls? What elements of communication must be learned and applied so that they will continue to talk to us?

"I always know which adults I can trust and want to talk to. I don't know how exactly—it's just like they send a message to my brain that says they care and they respect me. They make me feel good about myself. I don't mind trusting them with my feelings because I know they won't yell at me, make fun, or say, 'Everyone goes through that—it's just a phase.'"

Effective communication is imperative if we are to bring down the walls young people build around themselves. Three essential elements of open communication are *love, respect,* and *trust.* When these are present, teenagers will *want* to talk to us, and the walls will come tumbling down.

1. "I love you."

A teenager told us, "I wish my dad would hug me more and show affection to me when something's wrong or if I'm having a bad day. He used to do so when I was growing up, and it was a good feeling. It's not that I doubt my father's love, it's just that sometimes I need him to tell me he cares for me no matter what I'm doing. I don't feel a lot of love inside of me right now."

Perhaps the reason some parents and leaders have difficulty talking with teenagers is the way love is communicated. Usually we tend to take on more of an authoritative role. We exercise authority over young people, demand accountability, and then, if they comply and put together a good enough track record, finally convey our approval and love. That is not how God approaches us as his children.

Our caring and love must be constant and unconditional— given first, and given freely through good and bad, transgression or testimony, brilliant success or utter failure. Regardless of their choices, teenagers need our nonjudgmental love.

One young man finally gathered the courage to go to his bishop and confess several sins from his past. At the end of the interview, the young man said, "I feel embarrassed about unloading all this on you. What do you think of me?"

Without a pause the bishop said, "I love you for it. There isn't anything you could share with me that would cause me to love you less." The young man and his bishop enjoyed not only open communication afterward but also a deep friendship from that time forward.

We attended a youth conference in Arkansas where young people came from many different stakes, and no one seemed to know any one else. Everyone was feeling a little insecure and uncomfortable.

At the back of the cultural hall, we noticed a boy with fully grown hands on the ends of stubs at his shoulders, but no arms. Everyone walked past without looking at him. You could almost sense that each one was thinking, "My mom told me not to stare at people like this." That day we learned that the opposite of love is not hate. Rather, it is indifference. Even hate recognizes that someone is standing there.

We wondered, "How are we going to involve this boy?" On the other side of the cultural hall, we saw another boy who stood alone. He was heavyset and obviously feeling out of place. We said to ourselves, "This is perfect." Barbara went to get one boy, and Brad went to get the other. We met up in front of the stage, and Brad said firmly, "Now, you two be friends."

They didn't argue. They just said, "Okay." Those boys stayed together the whole conference. By the end, they had become good friends.

At the final dance, Brad was dancing in the middle of the dance floor when he suddenly felt that someone was staring at him. He turned, and there behind him stood the boy with no arms. Music was blaring and teenagers were dancing all around them, but the boy didn't move.

Finally he said, "Brother Wilcox, my friend and I want to invite you to our pizza party after the dance."

Brad smiled and said, "I'm honored. I'd be happy to come. You count on it."

The boy looked at his buddy at the side of the room, gave him a thumbs-up signal, and then turned back to Brad and added, "Brother Wilcox, we need a quarter to call and order the pizza."

Brad smiled and told him where his briefcase was, adding, "Find a quarter and go order us some pizza." The two buddies left excitedly, and Brad turned back to his dancing.

About half an hour later, Brad felt eyes staring at him again. Sure enough, it was his same friend. "Brother Wilcox," he said, "we

called and ordered the pizza like you said, but"—he hesitated—
"now we need thirteen dollars to pay for it."

Some pizza party! Brad thought. *They invite me to* their *pizza party, and* I *am buying.* He chuckled and told the boy, "You know where my briefcase is. Go ahead and pull out thirteen dollars."

Brad expected another thumbs-up signal and two excited boys to run off together. Instead, the young man just stood there looking at him. His eyes filled with tears. All he said was, "Really? You'd do that for *me?*"

Brad grabbed him and hugged him. Then he looked directly into his eyes and said, "Listen, you are worth so much more than thirteen dollars to me."

Unconditional love and caring can mean everything to young people. (Incidentally, Brad once shared the above story at another youth conference. Afterward, some of the group came up and said, "Brother Wilcox, we want to invite you to our steak and lobster party!")

Love is felt often but expressed rarely. As with faith, love must be made visible by works. In scripture we are counseled to love "in deed and truth." (1 John 3:18.)

One young woman wrote us a letter in which she talked about fighting with her mother and finally making up. "I wondered what I could say to make up with my mom," she wrote, "but I didn't have to think long because on Sunday, after testimony meeting, my mom hugged me and said, 'I love you,' and I guess our hearts could just feel each other's pain. Right then we knew we had forgiven each other."

Touch is one of the most important ways we have to express love. Unlike adults, most children welcome and even seek touch. Experts claim it is an actual need for children, one that is as essential as their need for food and water. But as adults, we try to convince ourselves otherwise, saying, "That's just not me any more. Touchy-touchy is not my style." Yet experts say that for adults, touching is also a primary means of communicating, whether we're conscious of it or not. We never outgrow our need for touching.

Dr. Brent Barlow, a professor at Brigham Young University and a professional marriage counselor, once gave students in some of his classes the assignment to go out and touch someone and then to come back and report. Some of the students said, "No way, we're not doing that." Some of the young men said, "People will think we're gay." And one student, a muscular football player, declared, "I will not do it."

Brother Barlow said, "This is an assignment, and if it is not completed, you will not receive a grade."

The football player repeated, "I will not do it."

At class the following day, the students reported on how they touched people and got positive or negative responses. Finally, it was the football player's turn. "I didn't touch anyone yesterday," he said. "But I knew you would flunk me if I didn't, so this morning I got up and looked at my roommate and—I hit him."

"Well," Brother Barlow said, "that's a start. Even a friendly slap on the back or a love punch is a form of positive touch."

Love is a natural component of our spirits. In the premortal existence we knew love and how to express it openly. Affection is not some freakish thing that is against our natures; it is part of the very core of our eternal natures.

Barbara always teases Brad that his motto must be "If it moves, hug it!" We are well aware of the cautions and guidelines given for personal and professional interactions. Even within Church organizations, there are certain callings given where hugging is discouraged. We understand the concern for appropriateness. Still, we have been among Spanish-speaking members of the Church enough to realize how natural and appropriate *abrazos* can be. We can't tell you how many young people, large and small, have just clung to us and hugged us until we could hardly breathe. We have seen teenagers wait in lines because they were hungering for the acknowledgment and acceptance that come with a simple hug. We have held teenagers like little children and rocked them back and forth in our arms as they have sobbed on our shoulders. We understand the need to respect personal space. But we know firsthand that sometimes there are more important needs that must be met.

One national survey revealed that 83 percent of the people surveyed grew up getting less than a hug a day, and 99 percent said they wanted more hugs. In another study, 81 percent of a group of LDS families considered to be very effective said they showed physical affection daily.

One missionary wrote to Brad from the Missionary Training Center: "Except for once with my father, I had never hugged a man before I hugged you—not even my brothers. I thought it would be weird, but instead it felt great. I appreciated it. It filled me with a glow that lasted through several days and literally carried me through my transition into the MTC." A girl wrote Barbara, "I had never had a hug from anyone in my entire life. I've wanted one. Oh, how I've longed for one, but I'm sorry because when I hugged you I didn't even know where to put my arms or anything. I'd never done that before—ever."

These young people were starved for something that has absolutely nothing to do with passion or sex in any way. They were starved for the validation and affirmation that come only through touch. Our friend Suzanne Hansen tells young people, "Remember you aren't making a sexual statement by giving a hug. You're making a statement about human love and caring. In the language of my Scandinavian forefathers, the Norse word *hugga* means to comfort, hold close, or console."

Jesus touched those to whom he ministered. "When Jesus had made an end of these sayings, he touched with his hand the disciples whom he had chosen, one by one, even until he had touched them all." (3 Nephi 18:46.) Is it by mere chance that certain things in the kingdom can be done only by the laying on of hands—including, very appropriately, blessings of healing?

Another essential expression of love involves actually saying the words "I love you." One girl wrote, "I believe my mom doesn't love me because I have never heard 'I love you' come out of her mouth for 16 years. I say, 'I love you, Mom' and she says, 'I know.' Is that normal?"

Mother Teresa, a woman respected around the world for her work with the poor people in Calcutta, is often asked, "What can I do? How can I help?" She points a finger at those who ask and says, "Go home and tell your families you love them."

"I love you. I'm proud of you. I've missed you. I'm lucky to have you." Such words are more important than we realize.

At a youth conference, Brad walked up to a young man and asked, "What is your name?"

The boy looked at him and replied, "Steven."

"Well, Steven, I'm glad you're here. I love you," Brad said, as he gave the young man a hug. It was obvious that the gesture scared the youth, and afterwards Brad felt that maybe he had come on too strong.

However, in a testimony meeting at the conference, Steven got up, with tears streaming down his cheeks, and said, "I've decided at this youth conference that I'm changing my life." He paused, then explained, "When I walked in here yesterday, I wasn't even sure if I was going to stay because I didn't see any of my friends. Then this guy who I didn't even know walked up to me and put his arms around me and said that he loved me. And if somebody who doesn't even know me can love me like that, I'm going to change my life."

After a similar experience at another youth conference, a young man wrote: "So few people hear the words I love you' these days except from outside sources that are merely trying to get them to lower their standards. I'm convinced that if more people felt and expressed love at home, there would be fewer teenage morality problems, fewer Word of Wisdom problems, fewer rebellion problems, and so forth. It's amazing what love can do for a person."

Some might question using a word as strong as *love* when addressing people we hardly know. Some may ask, How can we love strangers? But aren't we forgetting that, while we may not know each other now, we once knew each other well? By keeping an eternal perspective, it is entirely possible to feel deep love for someone we have not spent a great deal of time with.

2. "I trust you."

"I wish my parents understood my need for some freedom," a teenager wrote. "I want more privileges, and I'm willing to take on more responsibilities to get them. I wish they would realize that they can trust me more. . . . I wish I could really talk to them and tell them what's going on at school. I'm just afraid that they'll get all upset if I talk about sex and start thinking that I'm doing it and warning me about AIDS and stuff."

For open communication to occur, we must establish a

relationship of trust. One parent asked, "How can I trust my child? He is totally untrustworthy." The truth of the matter is, we don't have a choice. We can't follow teenagers around for the rest of their lives. In God's eyes are we, as adults, totally trustworthy? Yet Heavenly Father trusts us with many things, including his restored gospel. Perhaps he is giving us something to live up to—focusing on our potential as his children and not on our current problems. Our teenagers need the same message from us.

Some young people look at adults as obstacles to get around. But parents and leaders who establish relationships of trust are usually seen as people whom teens would never want to hurt or disappoint. One young friend, Todd Seamons, told us that when others would invite him to participate in questionable activities while he was growing up, he would always say no. "It wasn't because of the punishment I might receive if I was caught," he explained, "but because I knew how much my dad trusted me, and how disappointed he would be if I ever broke his confidence."

Trusting relationships can be established by allowing for some freedom and by keeping confidences. Another way to gain trust has to do with complimenting young people. A bishop from Texas once asked Brad to deliver a special letter to a missionary from his ward who was in the Missionary Training Center in Provo, Utah, and wanted to come home. Brad went to the MTC and met with George D. Durrant, who was the mission president at that time. President Durrant arranged a meeting between Brad and the struggling elder in a small office down the hall from his own.

Brad went to the MTC, met the missionary, and promptly began listing all the reasons he should stay on his mission. He gave him the letter from his bishop and told him the youth were looking up to him as an example. But Brad wasn't getting through to the missionary.

As they left the room and walked into the hall, President Durrant came out of his office. Brad called to him, hoping that he might be able to say something to help. President Durrant came toward them and did not even wait for Brad to say the elder's name. He said, "Hey, I know you. I don't need to be introduced to you. You stand out in a crowd. Of all the missionaries here at the MTC, I have noticed you in the lines and meetings. You stand out from the rest."

The missionary's face brightened. President Durrant turned to Brad and said, "Look at the eyes on this missionary." Then, turning back to the elder, he said, "You have the eyes for missionary work!"

President Durrant looked at Brad again and commented, "You know, someday this missionary might be as cool as you and me." Then he walked back into his office.

Brad thought, *Cool! He called me cool.* Then he wondered, *How did he do that? How did he establish such trust in a matter of a few minutes? If he were just playing salesman or practicing some sort of manipulation technique, he might have been able to convince some green, homesick missionary. But how did he do it to me? It didn't take much. He only had a few moments to spend with us. But in that time he sincerely complimented both of us.* The missionary stayed on his mission, and Brad went home wiser.

Young people appreciate it when we notice nice things about them and mention them with sincerity. Superlatives like "greatest," "smartest" and "best" may run a little ahead of reality, but remember, expectations expressed are often the seedbed of dreams fulfilled. Let us speak the language of possibility and hope. Elder

Vaughn J. Featherstone has said, "Compliments aren't what we are but what we should be."

We destroy trust when we are sarcastic or cynical. Despite what the writers of comedy shows would have us believe, cutting remarks are not humorous or witty so much as they are hurtful and mean. When we criticize any person, we not only alienate that one person but also send a signal to everyone else that someday they will be next. There are already too many people in the demolition business; we need to be builders. Kind words offer safety and security in a teenager's fearful world.

At one youth conference, Barbara approached an adult man standing by three young women and said, "Do you feel lucky to be here with three beautiful women?"

Trying to be clever, he quickly asked, "Where? I don't see any." This leader destroyed trust when he had a perfect opportunity to build it. Couldn't he just as easily have responded by saying, "Yes, aren't they gorgeous?"

This same type of conversation replays itself so regularly in our experience that it is tragic:

"I'll bet you guys have a great football team." "What? These wimps?"

"This stake must just grow pretty girls." "Yeah, if you like big women."

"You have great youth." "When they're asleep."

"Tell me the first thing you think the girls notice about this handsome guy." "His big nose."

"Your son's sure going to be a dynamic missionary." "If he will ever get out of bed in the morning."

"You really do that well." "Not!"

Do we need to go on? Far too often, parents and leaders take the clumsy position of blocking the very communication doors we want our children to enter. It is only when we concentrate on lifting young people, pushing them before us, seeing them elevated above us, that we have the spirit that will engender trust. Young people may put up with put-downs, but no one appreciates "cutdowns." They may laugh and play along, but deep down, it hurts. They remember and replay hurtful comments for years.

We are told in scripture to strengthen one another in all our conversation. (See D&C 108:7.) Let's get rid of such phrases as "just kidding," "yeah, but," and "if." We must treat the young people in our family and the Church as tactfully and positively as we would any investigator to the Church, for, in a way, that is exactly what they are.

As a teenager, Brad was self-conscious about how he came across when speaking to groups. In one sacrament meeting, he was called on with no prior warning to bear his testimony. "After it was over," he remembers, "I was sure I had made a total idiot of myself. Then a note was passed down the aisle where I was sitting. I thought it was going to be from some of the other priests who were going to tell me how stupid I sounded. Instead, it was from Brad Allen, my priests quorum adviser. The note said, 'Good job. I sure love you.' His words couldn't have been more needed. They lifted me up more than he will ever know."

Brad kept that note in his wallet until it became dog-eared. And until he left for his mission, Brad turned to that priests quorum adviser with any questions or concerns he had.

3. "I respect you."

A teenager sadly lamented, "If my dad would just speak to me like a peer instead of like a little boy. He makes me feel dumb when

I say anything. He doesn't listen to much of what I say because he doesn't really think I could have anything important or worthwhile to say."

In a Relief Society lesson, the teacher expressed the anxiety she and her husband had felt several years earlier. The stake president had approached them and asked if, since they had a spacious home near the chapel, they would mind hosting a luncheon for visiting authorities during stake conference. They gladly agreed. The stake president then informed them that one of the authorities who would be coming was the President of the Church.

The sisters in Relief Society gasped as the teacher explained how she and her husband planned the menu, cleaned the entire house, and set out their best china. After all, the Prophet was coming to visit their home, and they wanted to show proper respect.

On the morning of the anticipated stake conference, they were putting the final touches on everything, their teenage son came downstairs for breakfast. He ate some cereal and then, knowing it was a special day, cleaned up his mess. He even rinsed the bowl and then left it in the sink.

The sister teaching Relief Society said, "When I went to the kitchen and saw that bowl in the sink, I exploded. I yelled at my son and gave him a talking-to he would not soon forget." Then the family left to attend stake conference.

Through the entire meeting, the mother kept looking at her son sitting there on the chapel bench. She knew she had overreacted. She felt guilty. She explained to her Relief Society class, "I realized that while trying so hard to show respect to the special man who would visit my home later that day, I had failed to show respect for another special man who lives there every day. Didn't my son deserve the same respect I was extending to the prophet?"

She reached across her younger children, tapped her son on his shoulder, and mouthed the words, "I'm sorry. Will you forgive me?"

The mothers in Relief Society that day left with a greater determination to show more respect for their children. After all, if the prophet came to our home, would we leave the TV on and, as he spoke to us, say abstractedly "Really?" and "Uh-huh" while keeping our eyes glued to the show we were watching? If he used improper English or mispronounced a word, would we correct him? As he spoke, would we be thinking only of what he needed to do better? Would we give him advice or a lecture? Would we interrupt him, yell at him, or say, "Not now, I've had a long day"?

The quality of our communication with young people will improve in direct proportion to the amount of respect we show them when they talk to us. One of the most obvious ways to show respect is by listening. Heavenly Father listens to our prayers. In fact, as we pray, he usually does quite a bit more listening than talking.

Effective listening requires time, intent, and a temporary suspending of judgments and advice. When people are upset or discouraged, they don't need solutions to problems so much as they need understanding sounding boards. Right answers are usually obvious.

Maybe you're thinking, "So, am I supposed to just sit there with my mouth shut?" The answer is yes. Silence can be a potent sign of acceptance. Face the speaker, keep eye contact, and nod occasionally to show you're awake. But stay quiet, and you'll be amazed at the quality and quantity of comments you are able to draw out.

Sometimes another effective listening response is to paraphrase in our own words the messages we hear. This shows we are understanding what the speaker means. We can also say such things as "I see" and "I understand," comments that show we are relating to what the speaker feels.

Another important way youth leaders can show respect for young people is to make an effort to know their names. God knows us individually by our names. When Heavenly Father appeared to Joseph Smith, he did not call him "Hey, you" or "Aren't you one of the Smith boys?" He called him "Joseph."

We often attend youth conferences with Clark Smith, a tall former basketball star. In a matter of a day, Clark will memorize over three hundred names. He'll know every young person by name. He'll pray for them by name. At the testimony meeting, Clark will write the name of each young person who stands up. Is there any wonder why he gets through to the youth? Is there any question as to whether he can keep control during his workshops?

How does he do it? We wish there were a secret memory trick or association game we could give you that was less confusing than simply remembering, but we have not found one. Here is what Clark does: First, he focuses on the teenager and consciously makes an effort to remember his or her name. Then he repeats the name, saying something like, "Good to meet you, Joan." When he sees Joan again, he repeats the name to himself, and when he is close enough to talk, he addresses her by name: "Hi, Joan." Then he introduces Joan to others: "Russell, meet Joan."

It may sound a bit contrived, but it works for Clark. Each leader can adapt ideas like this one to suit his or her own personality; the important thing is that we learn people's names.

A stake president in San Antonio, Texas, in releasing the stake young women's president, Judy Lunt, paid her the highest compliment when he said, "She knows every girl in this entire stake by name." And she really did.

"I love you." "I trust you." "I respect you." These are three vital messages we must give clearly to young people to allow for effective communication. They are also the same messages parents and leaders want to receive from young people.

One seminary teacher came to school to find the students had decorated his office. For him, it was better than a raise. One father found a card from his son left on his pillow, a gift that for him was priceless. Young people attending Education Week gave a baby shower for one of the speakers. Every parent and leader can have a similar experience. We can almost guarantee decorated offices, notes on every pillow, and more baby clothes than one baby can ever wear if we will remember one thing: If we want love, trust, and respect *from* teenagers, we must give these things *to* teenagers first and then give them again and again. Whether or not we receive pats on the back from others will not be nearly so important to us as the personal peace we will enjoy in knowing we are trying to be a little more like the Savior.

On Brad's desk is a piece of the Berlin wall, a small chunk of cement with about an inch-long piece of barbed wire embedded in it and some fading colors on one side. It may seem a strange choice for a desktop decoration, but Brad keeps it there to remind himself that even the highest walls can come tumbling down.

Keys to Action

To open up and maintain communication with teenagers, we must learn to communicate these messages with them:

"I love you."

"I trust you."

"I respect you."

If we want love, trust, and respect from them, we must first learn to give these things to them— and to give them again and again. Be genuine. If you are pretending, they will know it. In the long run, whether or not we receive pats on the backs will be not nearly so important to us as the personal peace we will enjoy when we know that we are trying to be more like the Savior and to do as he would do.

CHAPTER 6

Setting Limits

As we establish open communication with teenagers, there is a message of great love that we need to make sure they understand: that we as parents and leaders have high expectations of them. How can we more effectively and lovingly communicate the standards we expect them to live by? How can we help them to obey and yet keep them from resenting us?

"I wish I could talk to my parents about the guy who came up to me and offered me drugs." Have you ever tried talking to your parents about things like that? "Just once or twice, but nowhere near the number of times that things have happened to me." What keeps you from telling your parents what's really going on at school? "I don't know. I'm afraid they will get mad and blow up at me." What could your parents do to make you feel more comfortable talking to them? "I guess it's the attitude. They have to show a little interest and try to understand. They could talk to me one-on-one instead of when other people are around."

P eople who write books or give speeches on how we should communicate with our children are a bit like professional golfers," wrote George D. Durrant. He explained that professional golfers make what they do look so easy. But, he said, as many times as he has been shown how to swing a golf club, he still can't seem to get it right. The same is true of communicating with teenagers. We have all been told how to do it over and over, but when a teenager wrecks the family car, all the training goes out the window. Suddenly everything breaks down and we say, "What's your problem? Why did you do that? When on earth are you going to learn how to drive?"

Like learning to golf, communicating with teens takes patience, effort, and a lot of practice. Before becoming too discouraged with ourselves, we need to remember that even the pros have a bad day now and then.

One parent said, "All this talk of love and caring is great, but what about when your teenager is out of line? What about when he has done something wrong? Aren't you supposed to talk about rules and keep discipline?"

Young people need love, and they need standards. It is not an either-or situation. Expressing love freely provides a strong and secure foundation from which to enforce standards, and enforcing standards is really an evidence of love.

Author Stephen R. Covey claims that "to love without discipline is fairly easy, also to discipline without love, but to combine them—that takes character and fortitude."

It is no secret that, deep down, young people actually desire limits and boundaries. As much as they might say otherwise, they long for teachers and parents who can keep order. Karen, a 15-year-old from Woodland, California, said, "I am thankful for the standards and values my parents have given me. Other young people around me are not so lucky. I watch them, and they are not as happy as I am. I appreciate my parents for giving me high standards."

By setting limits, we offer teenagers the security, stability, and safety they need without blocking communication. Here are some suggestions for accomplishing this.

1. Set clear expectations.

Teenagers need to know what is expected of them. Sixteen-year-old Micah from Piano, Texas, said, "My parents teach me the black and white of things—no beating around the bush with them. They tell me exactly what they expect of me when it comes to the Word of Wisdom. They teach me clearly and then say, 'You have your free agency.'"

Most parents would say they *do* expect their children to obey. Often, however, they are only *wishing* for obedience because their expectations are not stated clearly and frequently to their children.

One 50-year-old man hesitated when he was called to teach a class of teenagers in Sunday School, but finally he accepted the call. The Sunday School president brought him some materials and said, "Good luck. The last two teachers were eaten alive." The next day at work, after the man told a friend about his new calling, the friend went out and bought a sympathy card and placed it on his desk.

When the man arrived home that evening, his wife said, "Don't let them get you discouraged. You have always worked well with the youth."

"Yes," he replied, "but that was when I was a lot younger than I am now."

On Sunday he was well prepared, and he greeted the class cheerfully as they entered the room. But during the entire class period the teenagers acted as if he were not even there. They talked about school and told jokes, and when he tried to settle them down and get their attention, some of them were downright rude to him. He felt totally out of control.

After church, he told his wife, "Those teenagers acted like

complete hoodlums." She listened to him describe the class and then asked, "Did they know where the fences were?"

"What do you mean?"

"It may sounds strange," she said, "but I think teenagers are a lot like cows. They'll wander as far as they can and get into all kinds of trouble unless there is a fence. Once they know where the fences are, they are usually content to graze in the center of the field."

During the week, the man thought about this comment. He visited each class member to learn their names and find out more about them, and he gave each one a brief assignment for the next class. On Sunday, he went to class prepared with his lesson and also with his fence. He greeted the young people as they entered the room and sat down, and then he said firmly, "While I teach you today, I expect you to listen, with no talking. If you have comments, please raise your hand and we'll hear them in turn. But we are learning about the gospel here, and that is important. It is essential that I have your attention."

What was the man's report to his wife this week? Were the teenagers all wonderful? Did they all sit quietly with their arms folded? Did everyone live happily ever after? No, but things went better than they had the week before. The fences that the wife mentioned are the clear expectations and limits we need to set for our teenagers. He told his wife, "I had to remind them to be quiet several times, and I had to wait and not continue until they were with me, but I made it through my lesson. Two girls even came up after and thanked me." It was a small but crucial victory.

2. Maintain consistent accountability.

How many times do we state an expectation, or set a fence, but fail to follow through? We agree on a curfew with our teenager but then let it slide when he doesn't make it in on time. We tell the class to listen but then we keep on giving the lesson whether they are listening or not. One survey of high school students found that only 17 percent said their parents were consistent in their discipline. Once we set an expectation, we must insist on getting the behavior we expect.

A young woman admitted to her teacher that she had plagiarized a paper. The teacher thanked her for her honesty but explained that her grade would still have to be lowered and that the work would have to be redone. The girl was upset. She had been let off the hook so often for telling the truth that she had come to look upon honesty as just another strategy to avoid natural consequences. If we do not require that broken windows be replaced and stolen merchandise paid for, we too are stealing—robbing young people of a vital and important part of their repentance.

When several young men arrived late at a stake dance, the chaperon smelled alcohol on them. These young Latter-day Saints knew the standards of the Word of Wisdom. They knew the rules of conduct at Church dances. Since they were considered leaders in their local high schools, other young people at the dance watched carefully to see what would happen.

Their bishop kindly asked them to leave and escorted them out of the building. Because they were in no condition to drive, an adult leader volunteered to take them home.

The young men protested, saying they were sorry, they hadn't drunk all that much, and they would never do it again. But when their words had no effect on the bishop's decision to send them home to their parents, they became angry. The bishop calmly reminded them that *they* were the ones who had chosen this consequence; if they should be angry at anyone, it was at themselves. His actions showed how much he really cared—enough to risk his good relationship with them by standing firmly to uphold standards.

3. Express appreciation generously.

One observant teenager said, "My parents are quick when it comes to punishing me for disobedience, but they are pretty slow to reward me whenever I do something right." The scriptures tell us, "In every thing give thanks." (1 Thessalonians 5:18.) When a teenager lives up to expectations, we must express our gratitude.

One father said, "I never even thought of thanking my children for the little things they do. I guess I just expected them to do those things naturally. But I decided to try it. We had set a family goal to have less fighting, and I specifically asked the children to stop saying 'stupid' and 'shut up' to each other. Several days later, things were going pretty well. I went to each child to express my thanks for the use of better language in our home, and I couldn't believe the response. I thought they would think I was treating them like little babies. Instead, they seemed happy I had noticed their efforts. My teenage daughter even put a note in my car thanking me for being such a great dad."

4. Correct in private.

When problems with teenagers occur, it is best to deal with them in private rather than before peers, brothers and sisters, or other adults. If we let ourselves get into power struggles with teenagers in front of others, we will likely lose. Most teenagers would sacrifice their relationship with us long before they would ever allow themselves to look weak in front of other people.

Seek a quiet time, such as just before bedtime. Pick a

comfortable setting, one free of distractions or interruptions. In planning what to say, make sure that you have cooled down. Think of yourself as a consultant rather than a manager, a coach rather than a critic. Think of the conversation as an exploration rather than an accusation. Start by asking "What happened?" or "What's wrong?" rather than "I know you've been lying to me, and I want to know why."

Your teenager may say, "Nothing happened." Such a response is usually just a test to see if you really care enough to ask again. Don't give up. Keep the conversation going or wait in silence. If you are still met with a blank stare or a "not me," follow the direction of the Spirit.

Joy Saunders Lundberg wrote of one such time with her teenager: "Our son came home from school one day and seemed discouraged. I said, 'What's up? You seem down.' He replied, 'Jim [not his real name] is such a jerk.' And I asked, 'Oh, how's that?' I was surprised at what followed. 'He's been inviting his girlfriend over to his house every day after school since his mom started working.' Resisting the temptation to expound a magnificent sermon on morality, I said, 'Hmmmm.' And he said, 'It's so stupid. He's just asking for trouble.' Definitely similar to what I would have said, only more concise. I asked, 'What do you mean?' Then a flood of information poured forth regarding all the dangers of being alone in a house with a girlfriend. But it didn't stop there. He covered every base, including the terrible effects of venereal disease and abortion. All I did was listen and agree. I'm convinced he would have heard very little of the sermon had it been preached by me."

Correcting in private allows us to help teenagers reflect on what has occurred ("What went well?" "What didn't go so well?").

We can guide them toward value judgments ("Is that helping you?"), and help to formulate a new goal or plan of action for the future ("What do you think we ought to do about it?"). In this way we can stop having to play the role of the all-knowing dictator and simply start helping teenagers help themselves. Our job as parents is not to solve all of our children's problems for them, but rather to give them opportunities to begin solving their own problems.

If the situation requires discipline, remember that the word *discipline* comes from the word *disciple,* which means "a learner." Discipline, then, is teaching, training, and learning. It is not something we do to a child; rather it is something we do *for* a child.

The professional golfer says, "Just keep your head down and your left arm straight as you swing." This sounds simple enough. Still, when we try it, it just doesn't seem to work for us. We lose golf balls more often then we ever get on the green. But we're working at it. We're better than we used to be. We may never win any championships, but we might just win a match when it matters the most. We're trying, and that counts in communication just as much as it counts in golf.

Keys to Action

Young people need love and they need standards. Here are some suggestions for giving them both:

1. **Set clear expectations.** *Let them know what is expected of them. It may be difficult to believe, but teenagers actually crave guidance and direction. Setting limits for and with them shows them that we love them.*

2. **Maintain consistent accountability.** *Once we have set an expectation, we must insist on getting the behavior we expect.*

3. **Express appreciation generously.** *When young people live up to established standards, we must express our gratitude to them. They need to know that we notice their good behavior and not just the bad. This will also help them to want to live up to their standards.*

4. **Correct in private.** *If we must correct teenagers, we should show respect for them and do it in private. This allows us to help them reflect on what has occurred, to help them make value judgments, and to help them formulate a new goal or plan of action for the future.*

CHAPTER 7

Pressures and Stress

It is vital for us to realize that teenagers often experience negative stress and many pressures—both internal and external If we fail to correctly identify the particular pressures in the lives of those teenagers whom we love, we won't be able to effectively help them function in a world of complexities. What stresses and pressures most affect youth today?

"I wish adults could understand how many pressures are on me at school and how it's really a lot harder than they think. I don't know how to explain it. You have to try to do everything right and not look too stupid. You have to try to fit in. It gets really hard."

Do teens have pressures and stress in their lives? The answer is a resounding yes, and these pressures and stress can cause parents and leaders to hover on the edge of panic themselves, worrying about the possible effects of such problems on young people.

What is pressure? There are as many different answers to this question as there are people who have experienced it. But, quite simply pressure is any external force that influences us. Such forces may include friends, family, school, media, and change in our lives, however minor. Stress is an internal reaction to those outside pressures. It affects health and happiness.

Stress is an unavoidable fact of life. It is how we handle stress that makes it positive or negative. When the heat is on, do we turn it into a refiner's fire or just let it burn us out?

It is important to remember that though we usually speak of pressure and stress in negative ways, they are a vital part of why we were sent to earth. Positive influences, such as the Church, good friends, and family support, help us progress and improve. Stress can keep us motivated and productive. It often allows us to concentrate, focus, and perform at peak efficiency. Without it, we would likely become bored and frustrated.

What external pressures most affect young people? In one study, when adults were asked to name their children's top anxieties, they mentioned nuclear war, terrorism, being kidnapped, and the possibility that the parents might be divorced. When young people were asked what their principal worries were, however, the top responses were not having enough friends, being teased or bullied, and being embarrassed in front of their peers. The study reported that teens fear humiliation in front of peers more than having to undergo surgery.

As children grow, the influence of peers becomes a most serious matter. One mother wrote:

"We are having some anxious moments with our teenage daughter. We have spent much of the school year wondering what tricks she will pull next. They aren't your usual teenager acts of rebelliousness. They are mischievous and quite out of the ordinary. We have talked to her about free agency. She knows Church standards. She has even said tearfully that she wants to try to be better. But she has a friend who seems to have total control of her. Whenever there is trouble, this friend is not only in the middle of it, she is the instigator of it. And our daughter just goes along with anything her friend suggests.

"One day they skipped school while I was away from home. They brought several other kids to our house and had a party.

There was beer and there were boys, and you can figure out the rest. My husband, for some reason, decided to come home in the middle of the day to get something that really wasn't crucial. He just felt that he needed to go home. He found them all at the house. They scrambled to get out and left behind an awful mess, but he was able to stop the party before it went any further. When we later confronted our daughter about the party, she said that it was all her friend's idea—that her friend 'forced' her into it. Her need for acceptance by her friends and her desire to be popular with the boys are consuming her."

Our friend Jack Marshall read of an experiment that had been conducted having to do with peer pressure. The results were so startling that he replicated the experiment in his seminary class to see for himself. He drew a star, a circle, an oval, and a square on the chalkboard. He then invited one student to leave the room. The other students were told that when he pointed to each shape they were to name it correctly except for the square. "When I point to the square," he said, "you say it is a triangle." He then invited the student who was waiting outside to come back into the classroom.

"We're going to give you a little test," Brother Marshall began. All eyes were on the student, who began to feel nervous. Brother Marshall said, "Class, please name these shapes as I point to them." They chorused, "Star, circle, oval, triangle." The student standing at the front of the room began to laugh. He knew the final shape was a square. No one else laughed. Again, he felt uncomfortable. The class named the shapes several more times. Each time, the student at the front looked more puzzled.

Finally Brother Marshall told him, "It's your turn now. Name each shape as I point to it. Trust what you know to be true." Brother Marshall pointed to the first shape.

"It's a star," the student said.

"That's right. Now, the next one."

"Circle."

"And the next?"

"Oval."

"You're doing great," Brother Marshall said. "One more to go." Then he pointed to the square. The pressure was on. The student hesitated. He looked around the room. Some of the most popular students in the school were in that class. He shifted awkwardly. Brother Marshall said, "Come on, you know what this is. Go ahead and name it."

Quietly, the student said, "It's a triangle."

Brother Marshall couldn't believe it. This student had done exactly what the subjects in the original experiment had done. He expected the other students in the class to laugh as if this were a joke, but they sat in stunned silence. In a matter of minutes, they had watched a fellow student totally abandon the truth to fit into the group. They had seen the effect of peer pressure.

The influence of peers on teenagers is great. Still, it is only one of many external pressures with which young people deal. Changes and choices are encountered constantly at school, home, work, and church. When pressures are not dealt with appropriately, young people can become irritable, exhausted, overwhelmed, and depressed. This opens the door for many other problems.

In the back of the first book that Barbara wrote, she added a little note to teenagers who might read it and said, "If you have any problems, please write to me." She gave an address where she could be reached. She was amazed at the response. Barbara admits that when she first began reading through these letters, she thought the task of understanding the problems of teens would be easier than it is. As she read letter after letter, she felt that she was getting a pretty good picture of the anxiety, tension, and depression they faced. She thought she could just make a small list of problems that surfaced and then offer a tidy solution for each one. She says, "I was more than a little naive."

As she read the letters, she was surprised at how confusing it all started to become. Cause and effect were not clear. What caused these young people to drink? to turn to drugs? to experiment with sex? to consider suicide?

The more she read, the more she realized that the problems are all interrelated. One thing will lead to another and then another with no set order. Soon the starting point is unimportant because the problems are interwoven into a web that captures the teen's mind and body. It becomes nearly impossible to escape such a web unaided.

To illustrate, we have included sections from four letters Barbara received. From just this small sampling, you can see Barbara's dilemma in attempting to pin down exactly what pressures are at work in these teens' lives.

1. "I'm extremely overweight, ugly, and I have already lost my virginity. I am five foot four and I weigh 209 pounds. I slept with my boyfriend who was 17 at the time. I regret that day, and I probably will until I die. The guy turned out to be a real jerk. All of my friends know about it, and they are constantly asking me if I regret it. It's hard to talk about it with them because I feel so dirty and guilty. I am also very shy. My mom is so overly protective that it drives me crazy. Some days I look in the mirror and think I look kind of pretty, but most of the time I look in the mirror and say, 'Why am I even alive?' Lately I've been really depressed, and today I thought about committing suicide."

What's the problem? Obviously, this young woman is feeling guilty about her immoral choice. But what led to that choice? Why was she so desperate for acceptance? Has she a poor self-image because of her weight problem, or does she have the weight problem because of her poor self-image? She claims to be shy and overprotected. Is there anything to those claims or is she just avoiding responsibility for her own actions by blaming others?

2. "Over the last three years, I've tried everything to make people like me. I thought people didn't like me, so I turned into an anorexic/bulimic because I thought people would like me if I were skinny."

This girl's problem is an eating disorder, but what has caused that? It appears that she has a strong need to feel accepted, but why is this need manifesting itself in such a negative way? Can't she find acceptance in doing positive things? Obviously there are deeper problems that she is not sharing.

3. "All my life I've been worried about what other people thought about me. Then I started to think that the only way I could get attention and have friends was to be smart. So I started to do everything I could to get the best grades. I started to skip other activities to study for a test. One thing led to another. I started cheating and snooping around the teacher's desk for answer keys. School soon became my life. I never had time to write in my journal or read scriptures. I left my church friends alone."

This young woman is looking desperately for attention. She has turned good behavior—trying to do her best in school—into something self-destructive. She is focusing so heavily on one aspect of her life that everything else is getting out of balance. She is cheating so overtly that it is almost as if she is begging to be caught. Whose attention is she after with these actions? Is she seeking to impress peers? Is she crying for help from teachers or parents?

4. "Everything started in the seventh grade. I was very popular, played sports, and got great grades. I had nothing to complain about. Then I went into a really deep depression. I can't tell you what could have triggered it. Some things were not too great at home. I was just like any other girl my age except that from the time I was very young, I always hated myself. I never thought my parents loved me. We were never close. The last time my mother and father hugged me or told me they loved me was—I can't even remember. That summer I was introduced to something I had never felt before. It made me feel good when nothing else could. I wasn't so much into drugs, but I loved wine coolers. Boy, I could be feeling good with only one. I changed a lot. I became so depressed that all I did was come home and stay in my room. My parents never knew about my problem—and they never will."

Barbara read these letters and others like them and asked herself, What are the answers? What can anyone do or say to help? Do suicidal urges cause drug use—or does drug use cause a desire for suicide? Is immorality encouraged by peer pressure alone—or does family conflict also enter into the choice? Pressure can lead to poor choices and poor choices lead to more pressure. The whole thing becomes a downward cycle.

The pressures and stress young people face are real and solutions are not easy. It is a sticky web of worries. Nevertheless, there are things parents and leaders can and must do in order to help.

When Barbara was in eighth grade, she experienced something that allows her to relate to how many teenagers feel. "My best friend, Lynne, and I had not been socially accepted in the school," she remembers, "so we spent a lot of time together doing homework, studying for tests, or just talking on the phone. We were both good students, and by the end of the first six-week period of the eighth grade, we were the teacher's pets. For Lynne, studying and grades came so easily. Every paper she turned in came back with an A-plus at the top. But for me every homework paper and every little test was a struggle. Somehow deep inside of me there was a tremendous pressure to excel at everything, and so, in order to keep up, I started cheating on tests, with Lynne's help (after all, she was my best friend). I began pushing myself to my physical limits, and I started getting sick to my stomach each morning. This went on for a number of weeks. My parents were concerned and took me to various doctors. At one point, they took me into the doctor's office in a wheelchair. It had become serious."

Essentially, doctors finally diagnosed Barbara's problems as inability to cope with the expectations of perfection that she had created for herself. Her parents were confused. They had spent a lot of money on tests and doctors, trying to find out what was physically wrong with her, only to discover that it was something she had brought on herself—a psychosomatic illness.

Barbara's parents felt at a loss as to what to do next. Broken arms can be put in casts. Sick children can be given medication. But what were they to do with a daughter who couldn't deal with stress? Barbara says, "That year my parents and I learned some things that really helped me. It was not until we realized what the real problem was that I could effectively deal with this problem— with my parents' support. I still had the stress, but I didn't let it destroy me physically because I understood it. I found out that stress may be *a part* of life, but it doesn't have to be a *way* of life."

CHAPTER 8

Teaching, Loving, and Laughing

In a world of opposition and troubles, teenagers need all the help they can get. We can make a great difference in their lives, alleviating much of the unnecessary pressure, loneliness, and pain. What are some ways in which we can do this?

"I'm a freshman in high school. My parents and I never really get along. They disapprove of my friends, and they won't let me go out with them. My parents take everything away from me. They don't trust me, and I feel like they hate me. I used to be a straight-A student. Now I just don't care about anything anymore. I find myself becoming withdrawn, sleeping a lot, and not eating. I cry too often. I hate myself and hate life."

Remember the movie *The Wizard of Oz?* Dorothy found herself traveling a road through an unfamiliar world. She was met with many challenges and problems. But she encountered three friends who helped her find her way home—the Scarecrow, the Tin Man, and the Lion.

Young people today are in much the same situation as Dorothy. They are trying to follow a straight and narrow path through a world full of opposition. They need true friends to be involved in their lives if they are going to make it back to their eternal home. What part are we going to play in our teenager's journey? Are we going to be the Scarecrow, Tin Man, and Lion? Or are we going to be more like the Wicked Witch of the West, who appears long enough to torment Dorothy and then furiously flies away on her broom?

In the movie, the Scarecrow wanted a brain, which would help him to think; the Tin Man wanted a heart, which would allow him to show emotions, such as love and laughter; and the Lion wanted courage, which would make him brave. In helping teenagers deal with pressure and stress, we can play the part of the Scarecrow by teaching them to think things through and manage their stress appropriately. We can play the part of the Tin Man by exhibiting the emotions associated with the heart, including a sense of humor. And we can play the role of the Lion by helping them to face their problems courageously through learning about and emulating worthy heroes.

1. Teach youth to THINK about managing stress.

The ability to think through a problem and generate alternative solutions does not always come naturally. We need to teach young people to break a problem down into parts, focus on the most important parts first, and then solve the problem one step at a time.

When Brad was in graduate school, he and his wife often felt overwhelmed. As they mapped out their week's schedule, they frequently said, "Okay, we'll just have to take it one thing at a time." They chuckled one evening when their fourth-grade daughter pulled her homework out of her backpack and sighed, "I'll just have to take it one thing at a time."

It is also important that young people learn to think about the consequences of their actions ahead of time. If they are tempted to lower their moral standards and give time to fantasies, for example, they must also take time to think of the other moments that are sure to follow—not fantasies at all. Everyone loves fireworks on the Fourth of July, but few consider that on the fifth of July someone has to clean up the mess. Elder M. Russell Ballard explained, "We must govern our actions every day with our future in mind. One of Satan's clever tactics is to tempt us to concentrate on the present and ignore the future."

Have we taught children how to deal with stress by taking a break? Do they know how to appropriately escape for a while and how to have fun? What about the importance of exercise and nutrition? Barbara says, "The best way to teach relaxation is to relax with your kids. Play games, read a book together, or watch a video. Rather than just lecturing on the benefits of exercise and eating right, go on a family bike ride together and eat at a salad bar now and then instead of heading for an ice cream store."

One article we read claimed that the three best ways to reduce stress are: (1) stop smoking; (2) limit intake of caffeine; and (3) drink no more than four alcoholic drinks per week. We need to point out to LDS young people that simply by living the Word or Wisdom, they already have a huge jump on others when it comes to stress management.

Have we taught teenagers how to organize their time or study more effectively? Many of the pressures that come up and cause stress in their lives might be avoided with a little advanced planning. Barbara says, "One good way to teach effective planning is to involve young people in making plans for family activities, vacations, or youth conferences. It's also good to involve them in setting family rules and coming up with the consequences for breaking them." Teach teens how to use personal planners and how to calendar their time. Many go through their school years being told what to study but not how to study, and this can create problems and unnecessary stress. Stress can also be alleviated when they are guided as to how they should set priorities for their daily activities.

2. Teach youth to find HEART through humor.

This is always more easily said than done, but the truth is, if you can laugh at it, you can live with it. A sense of humor helps us overlook the ugly, endure the difficult, overcome the unexpected, and bear the unbearable.

The headline on a magazine cover near the grocery store checkout line read "Reduce stress: LAUGH!" Inside the magazine, an article told about many medical studies linking laughter with better physical and mental health. Humor helps. Humor heals. It's okay to laugh. In the Old Testament, Sarah said, "God hath made me to laugh, so that all that hear will laugh with me." (Genesis 21:6.)

Elder Boyd K. Packer addressed young men and women on one occasion and said humorously, "One day you will cope with teenage children of your own. That will serve you right."

A teenager at Education Week one year had hair that was trimmed nicely except for one swatch down the center of his head that must have been a foot long. Brad called him his "three-fourths missionary" and asked what he was going to do with the long hair when he entered the Missionary Training Center. He said, "My mom is going to have a big party and invite the ward. Then she'll cut it off, frame it and call it 'free agency.'"

We have met many parents who use humor to lighten stress. One mother wore a button that read "Be kind. I have a teenager." A father had a picture of a man begging for food and holding a sign that read "Unemployed." Next to it the father drew a picture of himself also begging for food and holding a sign that read "Two teenagers with cars."

Joy Saunders Lundberg wrote, "One evening my husband and I anticipated that our son and his girlfriend might arrive home a short time before we did, so we made a big sign that simply said, 'Smile, you're on heaven's candid camera.' Having fun can take the edge off parental supervision." Sara, a 15-year-old from Orem, Utah, asked her parents when they would allow her to begin dating. They said, "You're so pretty that we won't be able to let you date until you're at least 24!'"

Our friends Susan and Joe Shumway, who have eight children, tell about the time when Susan was expecting number seven, and they took their six little ones on a family vacation to Mexico. Joe had to leave early to get back to work, and Susan was responsible for bringing the family back home a few days later. "There I was, out of money and out of diapers," she recalls. "I was trying to keep track of all the luggage and all the children at the same time. I was so pregnant I could hardly walk." When she finally reached the customs counter, the man on duty there looked at her and then all her children and said, "Lady, go right on through. If you have drugs in those bags, you need them."

One man approached us after a parenting seminar and said, "Do you realize how a father's fears have changed through the years? The thing that used to keep fathers awake nights was that their daughters might pierce their ears and dye their hair. Now the thing that keeps fathers awake nights is that their sons might do the exact same thing."

Our friend Douglas Bassett told of a student in his seminary class who felt nervous because she had not studied for a test on pregnancy and prenatal development for her health class. She surprised herself by doing better than she expected on the test. In fact, she was so excited when she got on the school bus that afternoon that she yelled across the bus to her friend, "Hey, Sarah, I passed my pregnancy test!"

Brad's father-in-law was a busy bishop all through the years that his children were growing up. Because of his schedule, one Christmas the family didn't get to go shopping for a Christmas tree until all the nice trees were gone. They picked out the best one left on the lot, but when they got it home, they realized it was the ugliest Christmas tree they had ever seen. The children were frustrated and upset, but the parents chose to handle the situation with humor. Brad's mother-in-law said, "If we can't have a pretty tree, let's at least have a fun tree." She had the family members brainstorm, and they finally decided to make their Christmas tree a representation of the tree of knowledge of good and evil in the Garden of Eden. The children covered the tree with apple ornaments and red ribbons, and wound a stuffed snake around the trunk and propped its head up near the top of the tree. The older boys cut fig leaves out of green paper to hang on the branches.

Brad's father-in-law said, "Word of our tree traveled fast. We had lots of visits that year from members of the ward, and we soon realized they weren't there to see the bishop. They were there to see the tree. Even strangers came to look at it. It's the Christmas tree the family has always remembered best."

3. Teach youth to learn COURAGE from worthy heroes.

Who are the heroes young people look up to? *People* magazine for June 27, 1992, reported that the top teen idols of all time were

(1) the Beatles, who John Lennon said in 1966 were "more popular than Jesus," (2) Madonna, who was quoted as saying, "I saw losing my virginity as a career move," and (3) Elvis Presley, who died of a drug overdose.

No wonder one young woman said, "Being a total hero isn't possible in today's society." In a special summer/fall 1990 issue of *Newsweek,* a popular movie maker reportedly said, "I believe we are at a fairly frightening, transitional stage of history. We tried the Ozzie-and-Harriet thing in the '50s and that didn't work. Then we tried the hippie peace-and-love thing, and that didn't work either. Then we tried the yuppie thing, and the world got worse. So what's next? Today, there is no clear way for teenagers to go. All they have are politicians, TV preachers and cynical heavy-metal musicians telling them things that they sense are lies. No one is offering them the truth they crave so deeply."

We wholeheartedly disagree. Today there is a clear way for teenagers to go, and beyond the counterfeits and media-hyped imitations, there are worthy heroes to be found and followed. Many in the world may not recognize it, accept it, or appreciate it, but "the truth they crave so deeply" has been restored and is readily available. We can offer young people worthy heroes within the Church and in pages of the scriptures. We can fill our homes with pictures of these heroes.

At one youth conference in California, we asked the teenagers to tell us what pictures were on the walls of their bedrooms. Some said they had athletes; others mentioned rock stars and movie stars. We then talked about selecting worthy heroes. After the conference a letter of thanks came from one of the leaders. However, the words that meant the most to us were not written in the letter but across the back of the envelope: "P.S. Remember the new con-

vert you met named Billy? I saw him in the LDS bookstore yesterday buying pictures of the apostles and Book of Mormon charac-
ters to put on his bedroom walls."

One of Brad's heroes when he was growing up was President
Spencer W. Kimball. Brad says, "I will never forget meeting
President Kimball before my mission. I was touring in the cast of
the LDS musical *My Turn On Earth,* and we received word that
President Kimball was going to bring members of his family to the
play for family home evening. I was worried about it all week. You
see, I played the part of Satan, which meant I would be portraying
Satan in front of the prophet. What if he told me I did a good job?

"At the time, my church calling was teaching the 12-year-olds
in Sunday School. I asked the members of my class what they
would say to President Kimball if they had the chance to meet him.
One boy said, 'I'd ask him if he has to wear make-up in general
conference.' Another said he would ask him if he wanted to go
waterskiing with him the next summer. Finally, a Lamanite girl
said, 'If I had the chance to meet President Kimball, I'd just tell him
that I love him.'"

After the play the next evening, the members of the cast were
shown to a backstage room to meet President Kimball and some
members of his family. The production manager introduced Brad
as Elder Wilcox, because he was in the process of sending in his
mission papers.

President Kimball said, "Oh, Elder Wilcox, where are you going
on your mission?"

"I don't know," Brad said. "I thought *you* knew."

President Kimball laughed and asked, "What are you doing in
the Church right now?"

Brad said, "I teach the 12-year-olds in Sunday School."

President Kimball said, "There's no more important calling in the Church. What did you teach them yesterday?"

Brad couldn't remember. All he recalled was that he asked them what they would say if they had the chance to meet a prophet face-to-face. So he said, "President Kimball, I asked them what they would say if they had the opportunity to meet you."

"And what did they tell you?"

Brad smiled and said, "They told me that they would tell you they love you. I love you." Remembering the experience, Brad says, "And that's when he held me. He didn't just hug me, he held me for several moments. I will never forget the love I felt."

Teenagers do not need to meet a prophet to find a worthy hero. There are many very close to home. In Proverbs 4:18 we read, "The path of the just is as the shining light." A young man from Toronto, Canada, said, "Nothing gives me the courage to stand up to the pressures around me like knowing someone else is doing it too. I say to myself, 'If he can do it, then I can do it.'"

We have seen teenagers adopt the counselors at youth programs as their role models. These outstanding young adults are close in the age to the teens and have an impact that many adults can't have in the same way. As parents and leaders, we can be heroes to our teens as well. In the Book of Mormon, Alma told his son Helaman, "I would that ye should do as I have done." (Alma 36:2.) If how we live our lives allows us to be in a similarly strong position, we will influence the lives of young people.

Amy, a 17-year-old from Pleasanton, California, said, "My parents are my heroes. Their example makes me want to do what's right." Surveys have shown that teenagers' experiences with religious values in the home directly affect how they live these values in the community.

One young man wrote, "I just have one question for my parents and leaders: How can you go to R-rated movies and rent R-rated videos and then expect me not to do the same?" Another young man, Reid, age 17, from Piano, Texas, found an example in his father. He wrote, "My dad told me that he had never touched a cigarette in his whole life, and if I were to decide to try smoking he wanted me to invite him and he would smoke for the first time too. Because of that, I still have never touched a cigarette, and I never will."

Another young man wrote, "Life becomes so much easier as I draw nearer to Heavenly Father and Jesus Christ. They have done, and are doing, so much for me. I know that Jesus Christ died for me and that if I were the only person on the earth, he still would have done what he did—just for me." As our friend Kenneth Cope wrote in song, there is "never a better hero" than the Savior. The Lord is our ultimate example and guide, and he loves and will help every single teenager.

Just as in *The Wizard of Oz,* if we help the Dorothys in our lives to think their problems through, to gain heart by using humor, and to find courage through the lives of worthy heroes, they will have the support they need to continue down the road of life and ultimately make it home.

But wait! There is another character in the film that we are forgetting—Toto, Dorothy's dog. In fact, Toto is the driving force throughout the movie. The word *Toto* means total, complete, whole.

Young people must see that it is not enough to use intellect alone when dealing with the pressures and stress that confront them. Heart by itself is also insufficient. Courage without thought and feeling could end up causing more problems than it helps to solve. The goal that should drive us through the plots of our lives is the wise and sensitive combination of all these elements.

In the same way, balance is needed between our physical, social, spiritual, and intellectual selves in order to face the pressures and trials we encounter. When we are lopsided in any of these areas, our ability to deal effectively with even the smallest pressures is weakened.

Young people do not need any more wicked witches than they already have. They need friends who can help them be smart, happy, and brave. As parents and leaders, we must remember the positive influence of the Scarecrow, the Tin Man, the Lion, and—as Dorothy says in the movie—"Toto too."

Keys to Action

Here are some ways to really help teenagers cope with the stress and pressures they will face in life:

1. Teach youth to THINK about managing stress. We're often concerned about how our children are doing in their studies, but do they know how to study? Do they have a quiet, well-lighted place to study? Do they know how to manage their time effectively? Do they know how to relax and have fun? Negative stress is just as real and can be just as debilitating to teenagers as it is to adults.

2. Teach youth to find HEART through humor. Humor helps and heals. A sense of humor can help teenagers overlook the ugly, endure the difficult, overcome the unexpected, and bear the unbearable. Use humor with them instead of impatience and unnecessary reproach. Teach them by example and word to approach their own lives with more humor.

3. Teach youth to learn COURAGE from worthy heroes. Who are the heroes teenagers look up to? Whether we're aware of it or not, young people do emulate those whom they admire. Encourage them when they say something positive about a church leader or advisor. Help them to see these individuals as heroes. Teach them to look up to the prophets, and help them especially to emulate the Savior.

CHAPTER 9

An Umbrella Against the Rain

We know that teenagers today face many problems, but there are also ways we can offer them a system of support. What are some specific ways in which we can help them to make it through the storms of life?

R ecently we received a copy of the following letter, which a young woman wrote anonymously to her parents:

"How I wish I could tell you what has happened to me, but you know me only as your wonderful daughter, the Laurel class president who is popular, pretty, sweet, pure, and innocent. The pain inside me is almost unbearable. You see, while I was on a date a few weeks ago, I was raped. Oh, how I wanted to tell you, but I didn't want you to think badly of me. Now I'm so afraid that I am pregnant, but how can I ever share this with such wonderful parents—you, Dad, in the stake presidency, and you, Mom, in the Relief Society presidency? I would never want to hurt you in any way, so I have decided to keep the pain, guilt, and responsibility inside of me. How I wish that I could talk to you, and that you would put your arms around me, cry with me, and tell me that things will be okay. I love you both so very much."

A young man wrote, "The biggest problem for me—and I know this is true for a lot of other Mormons—is peer pressure. The other guys at school know I am a Mormon so they watch me constantly.

It's like they are just waiting for me to do something wrong. They are always saying, 'Come on, one drink. Do you think you're so much better than us?' Sometimes it's tempting—not the drinking, but the acceptance. I mean, I want to fit in. I don't want to feel like a total outcast."

These letters, which carry such great impact, illustrate why we feel so strongly about keeping the lines of communication between parents and teenagers open. It is essential that we be informed and aware of what is happening in teenagers' lives, and learn how to help them through these stormy times.

During a visit to Arizona, a Church Education speaker was invited to stay in the home of a young bishop and his family. The speaker met the small children in the family and also a teenager who was introduced as the bishop's sister. Later the bishop explained, "My sister is here with us because she got into so much trouble in her old school that my parents felt that it might be best for her to move to a new school and get a fresh start."

"How is it going?" the speaker asked.

"Oh, she has managed to get into plenty of trouble here too," said the bishop. "She has an addiction to crack. At first we wouldn't let her go anywhere without one of us with her. But my wife and I couldn't keep that up. It was killing all of us."

"So, how did you handle it?"

"I sat my sister down and explained that we were wrong to be watching her constantly. It was as if we had been keeping her in a box and feeding her through a little hole in the top. I told her that from then on, we were going to try to deal with her the way our Heavenly Father deals with us. He loves us, prepares us, teaches us, and then lets us decide what we will do and face the consequences."

The speaker was interested in the bishop's reasoning and asked, "How did your sister respond to that?"

"It's been stormy, but she is making it. Her progress is slow, but she is further along than she was."

Like this bishop, anyone who deals with teenagers realizes quickly that not only can't we stop the storms they face, we can't completely shelter them from those storms either. Perhaps the best we can do is to offer a support system—an umbrella against the rain. To do this, we must make every effort to be informed, interested, and in tune.

BE INFORMED

"I wish my parents would talk to me about morality and the Word of Wisdom," a teenager told us. "Whenever I bring up the subject, they just get scared. It's like they want to lock me up in the house and not let me go out. They don't realize that it's out there, and there's no escaping it. I just wish they would confront the issues I'm dealing with in my life instead of avoiding them and pretending that the problems will go away."

To be informed, it is important that we know what is happening in the lives of teens, that we recognize signs of stress in them, and that we know how to deal with our own stress as parents. Here are some suggestions that have proven helpful to us and other parents we know.

1. Know what is happening.

"My children didn't always make it easy for me to stay involved in their lives," Barbara remembers. "The day they became teenagers, they became social critics. Suddenly I could do nothing right. I didn't wear cool clothes and I didn't have a cool car. I also knew mothers whose children didn't want them to meet their friends. It seems they were an embarrassment to them. Experts say that such an attitude is to be expected. Still, rejection is tough to take. I wanted to pull away from my children, since that is what they seemed to want. But I thought about it and determined that sometimes what teens want and what they need are different things. I was their mother, and whether they admitted it or not, they still needed me.

"Don't get me wrong. I didn't follow them around with a video camera. But I knew who their friends were. I knew their class schedules. I knew their teachers. I found out what was going on at school. I learned the facts about drugs, alcohol, smoking, and the music my kids liked to listen to. When they watched TV or went to movies, I tried to keep up on what they were seeing. Adults will never be allowed to join the teenage world totally. That wouldn't even be desirable. But we can be informed enough that we know what is happening in their world."

2. Recognize signs of stress.

Some signs of stress are easy to see. Some are more difficult. Easy signs include fatigue, tenseness, restlessness, crying, inconsistent sleep and appetite patterns, frequent colds or headaches, persistent worrying, lashing out in anger, ignoring physical appearance, erratic achievement—good one week, poor the next. (Brad says, "That sounds like me in graduate school!") Most of us can relate. We know these signs from experience.

Signs of stress that are more difficult to spot and interpret are avoidance strategies, such as daydreaming or standing around on the sidelines and not getting involved in activities. Another sign of stress is passive resistance, when a teenager takes on an I-don't-care-so-nothing-can-really-hurt-me attitude. Another sign to watch for is when teens are constantly on the go. When they don't get enough rest and struggle with how to say no, it's a sure signal that stress is not being handled appropriately.

We know a young man who is intelligent and athletic. In his senior year of high school, he began faltering. His parents began to worry. Their son was within a few requirements of completing his Eagle rank in scouting, but suddenly he didn't want to finish it. He had the grades and test scores to receive scholarships from almost any university in the country, but he wouldn't fill out any applications. He was the first assistant to the bishop in the priests quorum, but his parents now had to drag him to church. His sudden lack of motivation bothered them a great deal. They pushed him harder, and he withdrew further.

A quorum adviser recognized the boy's behavior as a sign of stress. One Sunday the leader pulled the boy aside to talk to him. At first the boy was true to the "I-don't-care" attitude he had put on. However, the more they talked, the more his anxiety surfaced. He said that he would be graduating soon, and he didn't know what career he wanted to pursue. His parents expected him to attend college, but he thought general-education classes were a waste of time. He didn't want to finish his Eagle requirements because he knew he had made some mistakes and really wasn't worthy to be held up as an example to younger boys. He knew his mission was looming closer, and he didn't think he had a testimony.

After the talk, the leader talked to the boy's father and pointed out the stress the boy was experiencing right now. The father decided to back off for a while.

Slowly things improved. He finally completed some college applications even though he was too late to qualify for the scholarships he might have received. He attended church more regularly, though his attitude was still negative. Everything seemed to be going better except, interestingly enough, the boy's relationship with the quorum leader faltered. Now the boy wouldn't talk to him. He avoided eye contact with him and would rudely walk away whenever the leader attempted to say hello.

The leader felt bad. What had he said to offend the young man? Such behavior continued for weeks. Finally he realized that this too was a sign of stress. The boy had opened up to him, and consequently he knew things about the youth that no one else—not even the bishop—knew.

Sins that have not been resolved by repentance can cause a great deal of pressure and stress. An unworthy past that has not been properly taken care of can rob the present and future of peace, joy, and vitality. The leader concluded that one day, when the boy finally faces himself and God honestly, he may also be able to face him too.

3. Learn to manage your own stress.

One young woman wrote, "Sometimes my parents have a bad day and then they get upset and mad. I can understand this because I have bad days too—everyone does. It's just that when they are angry and snapping at me all the time, I begin to take it personally and start thinking the I've done something wrong." Another young woman wrote, "My parents need to realize that if they bottle up their financial problems inside of them, they may think they are saving the family from having to face them, but it's really harder that way. Their problems still affect the attitude of the family, but if mom and dad will not talk about them, then we don't know what is really wrong and we start thinking they hate us."

Part of helping teenagers deal with stress is to be aware of our own stress as parents. Few jobs are as stressful as parenting. Trying to balance demands of children, work, personal needs, and church responsibilities can seem endless and overwhelming. One mother said, "By the time I combine the lack of support I receive from my ex-husband with my financial worries and the myth of the 'perfect' family, I don't feel that I have anything left to offer my kids."

Another mother said, "I have to take some time for me. It is a pain and sometimes causes more stress than it relieves, but I have found that if I just take a brief time to exercise or read, I can turn my attention back to my children with better results." When parents let stress get the best of them, their children don't get their best.

Two young women wrote to Barbara about their home life. Consider how much easier it would be for these young sisters if their parents learned how to handle their own stress more appropriately.

The first writer said, "My mother has multiple sclerosis and has been in a nursing home since I can remember. My dad, because of this, has demanded perfection from me in everything I do. His comments about my never living up to his expectations have pushed me into drinking, drugs, and six attempts at suicide since I was 12."

The second young woman wrote, "I feel rejected at home. I'm seriously considering running away. My mother is never home because both my parents work. That wouldn't be so bad except my dad is always yelling at me and my two brothers to clean up our rooms or wash the dishes or vacuum while he just stares at those dumb football players in the dumb football game on TV. Our house never has the Christmas spirit, even on Christmas. This year my parents were so stressed out on Christmas Eve that everyone ended up in a bad mood."

Help is available for parents and leaders from many sources. Information on the topic of stress management is plentiful. However, as with many things, most of us already know what we should do. It's just a matter of doing it. As a Japanese proverb says, "If we simply deal with the problem, the problem becomes simple."

BE INTERESTED

"I would like to talk with my dad about girls and stuff because he is a guy, and I think he would understand," one young man said. "But I don't ever feel like he has time for me. When I say, 'Dad, can we talk?' he just rolls his eyes, looks at his watch, and says, 'Well, okay. So what's so important that we have to talk about it right now?' It totally kills my enthusiasm."

In dealing with pressure and stress, young people usually know what they should do. Like us, they may not need instruction so much as they need to know that we are interested in them and care about them. We can listen to them and allow them to talk out their frustrations. We can make a conscious effort to evaluate our own expectations and keep them realistic.

1. Listen with empathy.

Ruth stormed into the house and slammed the door furiously. The wall shook and the light fixture swung back and forth. Her father, a member of the stake presidency, wasn't usually home this early. To her surprise, Ruth heard him start down the hall from his study. She could tell he was upset at how hard she had slammed the door. But before he could give her his usual lecture about "don't break it unless you can afford to fix it," he saw her crying. He said, "Hey, what's with the tears?"

Ruth said, "I don't want to talk about it." She started walking past him toward her room.

He stopped her. "Come on, tell me what's wrong."

Ruth felt more comfortable talking with her mother, but right then she was so frustrated that she was willing to tell anyone. She turned to her father and sobbed, "It's just awful. There is this kid at school and he is really popular. He has been eating lunch with me and my friends. Well, he's not very good at math and stuff." Ruth was struggling to get the words out. "So I've been helping him with a big assignment that was due in Mr. Ivan's class, and the guy kept saying that he didn't understand how to do it. Yesterday he asked if he could have my answers. I didn't know what to say, so. . . ."

Her father picked it up from there: "You gave him your answers."

Ruth nodded and went on. "But that's not all. Mr. Ivan found out, and the principal put us both on academic probation. He said he's not going to let me graduate. The story has gone around the whole school now. It's awful."

Her father's first inclination was to criticize his daughter's actions. But he restrained himself and remained quiet. In his mind a small debate was happening. He was feeling two roles: father and priesthood leader.

The father inside him wanted to get upset and say, "Well, this is your own fault, young lady. You should never have given him your answers in the first place. I hope you learn a lesson from this." The priesthood leader inside him said, "How would I handle this situation if this were not my daughter but another young woman in the stake coming to me for advice?" The father in him was upset at Ruth for letting this happen, perturbed that she didn't have more backbone when it came to peer pressure, and concerned for Ruth's reputation as well as his own. The priesthood leader was feeling Ruth's pain, empathizing with her vulnerability, wanting very much to comfort her and dry her tears.

Ruth's father moved closer to his daughter and hugged her tightly. "Don't worry, honey. We'll get this straightened out. I'll call the principal tonight. Would you like a blessing?"

Ruth knew there would be consequences to face for her dishonest choice, but things finally did get straightened out just as her father said they would. Perhaps the best thing that came out of the whole experience had nothing to do with school. She later said, "I didn't want to tell my dad what happened because he has never been very good at listening. He's too quick with advice. But that day I found out that when I really needed him, my dad was there for me, and he really did understand."

Barbara says, "It's always easier to be patient and understanding if it's someone else's teen. Even with my own daughter, it was much easier for her to be best friends with her Young Women president and accept her advice. Sometimes young people feel safer talking with someone who is not close enough to react with shock or anger to the things they say."

In the same way, it's also easier to listen to the problems of someone who is not so close to you. For example, if the girl next door came over and confided that she was pregnant, most of us would try to be understanding and calmly help her see what her next steps need to be. We certainly wouldn't be yelling in anger or feeling hurt and betrayed. But if that girl were our own daughter, it would be more difficult to control emotions and personal reactions. The closer we are to the person, the more responsible we feel. According to Barbara, "That's why a good rule of thumb to remember is that when children talk over their problems with us as their parents, we need to treat them as well as we would treat our neighbor's teenager."

2. Have realistic expectations.

A schoolteacher in Georgia has the following rules posted on her classroom wall: (1) We are all learning here. (2) Making mistakes is okay. (3) You don't have to know everything today. (4) Intelligent people ask for help. Think how comfortable you would feel as a parent if your child were enrolled in such an environment. Now consider how comfortable Heavenly Father can feel about "enrolling" teenagers in our homes and classrooms. What guidelines are posted on our walls? What expectations are we communicating?

A young woman wrote the following letter: "I'm 15, and I feel like I'm trapped in a jail with my own family. I live with my dad, my older half-brother, and my younger brother. My sister lives with my mom in another place. My problem is that I don't know how to tell my dad that I have feelings too and that he is expecting too much of me. If I ask him if I can spend some time with my friends, he tells me to clean the house. I could ask my brothers to help, but they are like my dad and think that cooking and cleaning are women's work. My dad just sits in front of the TV while I work. I feel like I'm my dad's wife when I'm only his daughter. How do I tell him that I'm only 15? I can't do all this stuff by myself and keep up in school too."

Another young woman wrote, "I wish my parents would stop nagging me about little things. They should be grateful I'm such a good kid instead of always expecting more. I know I'm not perfect and that I have a lot of room for growth, but it seems like I can never please them."

While some teenagers may benefit from having their levels of anxiety increased by adults, the majority of them do better if adults will help them lower their anxiety levels. Words such as "It's okay, everyone makes mistakes," "Nobody is perfect," and "Just take it one step at a time" may seem trite to us, but they go a long way in helping teenagers.

3. Confront fears.

A mother told about a time when her son was asked to speak in stake conference. "He was terrified," she said. "He doesn't think of himself as much of a public speaker, and he hates big crowds. He is much happier being with animals than people."

As the big day drew closer, the mother recognized all the signs of stress. In fact, these weren't just signs, they were massive electric billboards. She tried to help. She was willing to listen, but he was in no mood to talk to her. She assured him that it didn't matter what he said in the talk; she was already proud of him for being willing to accept and fulfill this assignment from the stake president. Nothing she did or said seemed to help.

Finally, on the day before the conference, she tapped on his bedroom door. He said, "Come in." She entered to find him surrounded by scriptures, church books, and wadded-up papers. His tenseness and nervousness were obvious. She asked, "Look, what's the worst thing that could happen?"

"I'll make an idiot of myself."

"What can we do to handle that?" Her tone showed confidence in his ability to cope. She was treating his fear with respect.

"Well, would you listen to what I've written so far?"

She was surprised at the request. If she had suggested the same thing, he probably would have told her to get lost. She listened intently, praised him generously, and offered a few suggestions.

The following day the young man gave an excellent talk. His mother told us, "It was short but wonderful. He spoke sincerely of his love for the Savior. The visiting authority even commented on how well he did, which made him feel on top of the world. I was really relieved and happy that it turned out as a good experience."

Once "the worst thing that could happen" is out in the open, it can be demystified. Panic and fear become less intense. When teenagers are able to admit the truth and say the unsayable, the problem isn't solved, but the sting has been taken away.

BE IN TUNE

"My parents and leaders talk about peer pressure as if it is something that all the nonmembers gang up and put on the members," a young man said. "That is not the case with me at all. Every negative experience I have had with peer pressure has been from other Mormons who are not living the way they should."

When we are in tune with the Spirit, we can know how to help young people deal with the pressures they encounter. The Spirit takes individual circumstances into account. However minor or severe the problems, we should always encourage young people to draw strength and perspective from gospel teachings and lean on the Lord.

1. Draw strength and perspective from the gospel.

"If I didn't have the teachings of the Church, I don't know where I would be right now," a young man said in a testimony meeting at a youth conference. Many young people feel gratitude for the insights and answers the gospel provides for some of life's most pressing questions. One missionary said, "Without the doctrines of the Church, not only would I not be on a mission, but I would probably not even believe in God. If I weren't LDS, I don't know if I could sort through and make sense of it all. I think I probably would have just given up on religion altogether and joined the majority of people who wander aimlessly though life never knowing who they are or what their purpose is."

A recent convert was asked if joining the Church had solved all of her problems. She said, "No, but it has given me a new set of glasses with which to see them, and they just don't look all that insurmountable anymore."

Brad thought of this when Barbara wrote him a letter during a difficult and challenging time: "Brad, I am so sick about what has happened that I can hardly stand it. Every time I think of it, I want to cry again. But through my tears, I am absolutely positive that all things will work together for good. I can hardly wait to look back on this horrible time and say, 'I'm grateful for what happened.'

"Right now that seems impossible," she continued, but then she pointed out that she had said exactly the same thing when she had had another disappointment in her life. Afterwards, she recalled, "I realized that things had worked out for the best after all So, as hard as this time is, and as much pain as I have suffered, I can't help but wonder what good will come out of it. Sorry this letter is messier than usual, but the plane is going through terrible turbulence right now—how fitting."

The teachings of the gospel give us a deep well from which to draw strength and perspective when times get hard. When we sing the hymn "We Love Thy House, O God," we affirm the strength we receive from the gospel: "We love the word of life, / The word that

tells of peace, / Of comfort in the strife, / Of joys that never cease."
(Hymns, no. 247.)

What better stress management than to follow the gospel teaching to forgive ourselves and others? What more positive way to deal with stress than to pray for our enemies and those who trespass against us? When we partake of the sacrament worthily, we can erase mistakes of the past and start anew. In the gospel plan no one is expected to be perfect in all things right this minute, but we *are* expected to be repentant and willing to keep striving.

It is rejuvenating to lose ourselves in service, to study scriptures, and to enjoy moments of private prayer. When pressures mount, how reassuring to see them in the eternal perspective of the plan of salvation. The purpose of this life is happiness. We are meant to have joy. The Atonement of Jesus Christ can be a constant blessing in our lives.

It is strengthening to know that struggles and trials can be for our good, and that however difficult a particular trial may be, God will never allow us to be tested beyond our capacity to pass the test. We do not face any pressure and stress alone. God will never abandon us. Brad tells young people, "God did not remove the Red Sea, and He will help us through our problems too."

The one totally reliable antidote to stress in children is parents' love. How blessed are families in which love is felt and communicated. Doubly blessed are those who have a knowledge of the constant love of their heavenly parents.

2. Lean on the Lord.

A group of seminary students selected as their theme for the year "Lean on the Lord." If we will allow it, the problems and pressures of life can actually draw us closer to the Lord. As surely as we would lean on a friend when the road seems long and we feel weak, we can lean on the Lord. He has experienced this mortal life and understands and is always there for us. In these latter days he has said, "Where two or three [or more] are gathered together in my name, . . . there will I be in the midst of them—even so am I in the midst of you." (D&C 6:32.)

Joseph Smith experienced great pressure and stress throughout his life, but God supported and taught him through every hardship. One such occasion was when Martin Harris repeatedly begged Joseph to ask the Lord to allow him to show the pages of the Book of Mormon that had been translated thus far to members of his family. For a brief time Joseph apparently was more concerned about what Martin and his family thought than what the Lord desired, for he let Martin take the pages—and eventually they were lost.

The days after this were awful ones for the Prophet. He lost the privilege of translating, and he was angry with himself for giving in to Martin's demands. Finally, the Lord told him, "You should not have feared man more than God. You should have been faithful; and he would have extended his arm and supported you against all the fiery darts of the adversary; and he would have been with you in every time of trouble." (D&C 3:7–8.)

This message is one that young people everywhere need to understand. The Lord told Joseph, in effect, "I know peer pressure is great, but remember that if you're faithful, I will support you no matter how difficult the pressure and stress become."

Teenagers must realize that however stormy life's situations can be, they can draw closer to the One who said, "Peace, be still" (Mark 4:39), and find comfort. We can enjoy the internal peace of Christ regardless of external circumstances and pressures.

Barbara once told a group of young people about some trying times in her own life when, in desperation, she asked, "Heavenly Father, are you there?" and heard Him answer in her heart, "Yes, Barbara, I'm right here."

"I challenged those young people to go home that very night," she said, "and ask their Heavenly Father on their knees if He is there for them and if they were on the right track, and if not, what they should do to get on the right track." Some time later she received this letter from a young woman who had accepted her challenge:

"I just wanted to write you and tell you that I got down on my knees and asked my Heavenly Father if He is there. I stayed in that position a minute or two, and a quiet voice inside me said, 'Yes, Becky, I'm here.' Then I asked, 'Heavenly Father, am I on the right track?' After a minute or two, I heard the quiet voice again say, 'Yes, Becky, you're on the right track.' After I ended my prayer, I felt so good. But then I began to think that maybe my mind was playing tricks on me. However, I knew myself well enough to be able to trust what I was feeling. I wasn't pretending or making this up. I know it was my Heavenly Father answering my prayer. . . . Sister Jones, I grew up thinking I have a wonderful Heavenly Father who loves me and an Elder Brother who loves me so much that He gave His life for me, but now I don't just think that anymore. Now I know. No matter what happens throughout my life and no matter how hard things get, I know I am not alone."

The gospel of Jesus Christ, restored in its fullness, is our best umbrella against the rain. An 18-year-old youth named Jacob summed it up nicely when he wrote this message to parents and leaders: "First of all, you have to open your eyes and realize how bad it is everywhere—at work, at school, in public. People are swearing, telling dirty jokes, and doing bad things. Don't try to shelter us from that—hoping you can keep the world from influencing us. That's impossible these days. Instead, educate us and prepare us before it's too late. Don't let our reluctance and complaining keep you from encouraging us to do the right things. Teach us the gospel and keep us close to the Church. Help us put on the whole armor of God, as it says in the scriptures. Then we will be protected as we face the world every day."

Keys to Action

Just as we can't stop the storms that teenagers face, we also can't completely shelter them from the storms. The best we can do is to offer a support system, an umbrella against the storm. Here are some ways we can do this:

1. ***Know what is happening.*** *Be informed enough to know what is going on in their lives.*

2. ***Recognize signs of stress.*** *Such signs include fatigue, crying, restlessness, inconsistent sleep or appetite patterns, frequent colds or headaches, persistent worrying, lashing out in anger, ignoring personal appearance, erratic achievements (good one week, poor the next).*

3. ***Learn to manage your own stress.*** *Take time for yourself.*

4. ***Listen with empathy.*** *Handle your teenager's problem as calmly and patiently as you would handle the problem of your next-door neighbor.*

5. ***Have realistic expectations.*** *Most teenagers do better if adults help them lower their anxiety levels with such phrases as "It's okay, everyone makes mistakes," "Nobody is perfect," "Just take it one step at a time."*

6. ***Confront fears.*** *Panic and fears become less intense when worries are brought out into the open and demystified.*

7. ***Draw strength and perspective from the gospel.*** *Gospel principles provide a deep well from which to draw strength and perspective when times get hard. When pressures mount, draw on those principles.*

8. ***Lean on the Lord.*** *Heavenly Father and the teachings of the gospel are our best umbrella against the rain.*

CHAPTER 10

Three Levels of Testimony

How can we help teenagers to see that they have more testimony than they might think they do, and help them build upon their testimony? What are the different levels of testimony? What can we as parents and leaders do to nurture their faith and knowledge?

"I'm trying to prepare for my mission but I have found myself doubting, questioning and worrying. I don't even know exactly what I am feeling. It's like there is this huge black hole in my heart. I don't know what's wrong and I'm scared. Everything I hold dear is slipping through my fingers and everything I used to know for sure I don't know anymore. Where did my testimony go? Or did I just never have one in the first place?"

If a person has a problem with the Word of Wisdom, chastity, paying tithing, keeping the Sabbath, inactivity—whatever it is, that's not the problem; it's a symptom of the problem," according to popular youth speaker Jack Marshall. "The real problem is the level of the person's faith and testimony."

One of the best things we can do to build spirituality in teenagers is to help them strengthen their testimonies.

A mother told her home teacher, "James came home from church in tears."

"Why?" the home teacher asked.

"I'm not sure, but apparently they had a testimony meeting in the deacons quorum meeting today, and everyone bore his testimony except James. The other boys started pushing him, and I don't know what was said, but he came home crying."

"Too bad," the home teacher said. "Maybe next time I come we can have him practice standing up to speak so he won't feel nervous."

"No, I don't think he's afraid to speak before people. I think that the reason he didn't bear his testimony is that he is not sure if he has one."

Many young people feel like James. And many adults, like James's mother and home teacher, are concerned and want to help. Perhaps the first thing we must do is stop speaking about testimonies in light-switch terminology—on or off, you have one or you don't. Maybe a better analogy would be that of a gas tank: it can have countless levels of gas in it between full and empty. As Brother Marshall said above, "The real problem is the level." Just as the gas in the tank may be any one of many levels, so may the strength of testimonies be at different levels.

Young people like James usually have stronger testimonies than they realize. The needle on their gauge may not be pointing to full, but it's not on empty either. When considering youthful testimonies, the challenge is not that young people don't *know*. It is usually that they don't *know* they *know*.

Just as gas gauges usually have three marks between empty and full, there are also three levels of testimony between faithlessness and a perfect knowledge: experience, which might be likened to the quarter-tank mark; study, the half-tank mark; and revelation, the three-quarter-tank mark. (See Alma 32.)

1. Testimony of experience

"A lot of people at school think really weird stuff about the Church," a young woman said. "Like, they always talk about polygamy and ask me how many wives my dad has. And they think Church leaders or my dad pick the man I'm going to marry. They also say dumb things about the Church being against women or blacks, which is totally untrue. If people would just take time to get to know us, they would find out the truth."

The testimony of experience is gained as we participate in the Church and interact with Church members. We attend Primary, Mutual, and social activities. We go to sacrament meeting, where we partake of the sacrament. We worship the Savior and learn of Him. We shake hands, sing hymns, give talks, and are surrounded week in and week out by family, friends, and wonderful experiences. We know what it is like to be Latter-day Saints because we have experienced it firsthand.

Even the youngest children can bear a strong testimony of experience. Christ taught, "If any man will do his will, he shall know of the doctrine." (John 7:17.) Teenagers who "do" Church know much more than they give themselves credit for. This religious living gives them experiences with religious principles that, in turn, are influential in value development. Even if they have not yet received an intense spiritual witness, they can still stand and declare in all honesty, "I can bear testimony *from my own experience.*"

One year several non-LDS students from Europe came to Education Week with their American hosts. When Brad was introduced to them, he asked if they planned to attend the youth dance that evening. One of them, a young man from England, said, "I thought Mormons didn't dance."

Brad assured him that he was mistaken and that if he would attend the dance with his friends, he would have the time of his life. The next morning the young Englishman came running up to Brad and exclaimed, "I had so much fun! It was the greatest dance ever!" Then he added, "Now I *know* Mormons dance—can they ever dance! What's even better is that everyone was having fun without any alcohol."

Brad told him, "Some people say Mormons are the only people in the world who can have so much fun and still remember it in the morning." The youth laughed and said, "When I get back to England, I'm going to straighten out all my friends who told me Mormons don't dance because now I know they do."

This young man, though he was not a member of the Church, now possessed a certain level—though very limited—of testimony: a testimony of experience. After Education Week, Brad sent a referral card on him to the Church Missionary Department. Not long after that, he received the following letter from England:

"Dear Brad, I would like to thank you for sending the missionaries out to my home. They have visited three times, and I am becoming very good friends with them. It is really good to have them visit. I have attended one of the activities that they have arranged and will be attending another this weekend. I know it might sound a bit weird, but after a visit with the elders, I feel really good, but at the same time I just want to cry. It is a really strange feeling but at the same time it is a warm feeling."

The young man's testimony of experience was growing.

Another young man had been a member of the Church for only a few weeks when he was selected to represent his school in an all-state band and orchestra. He went to another city in the state, where the musical groups were scheduled to perform, and roomed with some other young men in a motel.

Late one night after he had gone to bed, the other youths began to talk. "I didn't like what they were saying," the recently baptized boy told us, "so I pretended to be asleep. But I heard them bragging about the drugs that they were taking and selling—one of them in an elementary school—the shoplifting they had gotten away with and the young women they had defiled. Suddenly one of the guys threw a pillow at me and said, 'Hey, I heard you just joined the Mormon church.' I said, 'Yeah, what of it?' He said, 'Well, my minister says that you are going to hell'"

Then the young man said, "I don't know a lot about the Church—I mean, I don't know the scriptures or the doctrine very well. But one thing I know for sure is that there is no way that those guys can be talking about selling drugs to little kids and sleeping around with different girls and then tell *me* that I'm going to hell for joining a church!" His testimony of experience had carried him through.

Most teenagers who claim their testimonies are on empty are usually sitting on at least a quarter tank, and they don't even realize it. Parents and leaders must help them to see that when it comes to their experiences in the Church, they are already expert witnesses of the truth.

2. Testimony of study

"I've always heard people talk about the Book of Mormon and quote from it and I've read parts of it for Sunday School," a teenager commented, "but it wasn't until I really started to read it straight through in seminary that I began to understand what was going on and how deep it is. There is so much there that I just overlooked. When I used the cross-references with the Bible, I saw for myself how the books go hand in hand and how either one, without the other, is incomplete. The more I read, the more convinced I was that the book could never have been written by one man alone, especially not Joseph Smith, a young man with very little formal education."

The testimony of study is gained as we learn the revealed word of God and find answers to our questions. Missionaries know the excitement felt by many upon hearing the plan of salvation for the first time. Such investigators sense that all the puzzle pieces are finally fitting together for them. Things they have felt all along to be true are then confirmed, and they discover new truths concerning what they had previously thought to be mysteries.

One year we were scheduled to attend a youth conference for the children of LDS military families in Japan. Joining us would be Clark Smith, Lorie O'Toole, and, as Barbara's special guest, Gretchen Polhemus, who had just completed her year as Miss USA. Gretchen had been introduced to the Church by Barbara and Barbara's husband, Hal. She responded very favorably. Still, she knew very little of what Latter-day Saints believe. As the time of the trip drew closer, Barbara became ill and finally had to cancel out.

The remaining members of the group flew to southern California from their various homes and boarded the plane to Tokyo. Brad sat next to Gretchen. He told her, "Most of the young people you'll meet at the conference will be Mormons, so it would probably be good if you found out what our Church is all about." On a small airline napkin, he outlined the Apostasy, Restoration, Book of Mormon time line, and plan of salvation. "This is fascinating," Gretchen said.

During the entire flight to Japan, the group talked and shared scriptures, and Brad continued to scribble things on the little nap-kin. As the plane finally landed in Tokyo, Gretchen picked up the crumpled, pen-marked napkin and said, "Yes, it makes so much sense. It's all so clear."

Gretchen loved the young people she met at the conference in Japan. She sensed something unique about them that she had not felt with any other group of youths she had met in her travels as Miss USA. She also saw in those young people something she didn't have.

The Church members in the group went to the Tokyo Temple to do baptisms for the dead. When Gretchen found out she could not go in, even to watch, she asked Brad, "Why?"

He explained, "It's like a graduate class at a university. It's not really closed to anyone, but to be able to get in and understand what is going on, you have to be prepared. Anyone can choose to go to the temple just as anyone can choose to go to graduate school. However, in both cases, there are certain requirements that need to be met first. Graduate school is open to anyone who is first willing to go to junior high, high school, and college, and then pass all the required tests."

Gretchen laughed. "So, I guess I'm still in elementary school!"

When the young people at the conference sang "I Am a Child of God," the Spirit touched Gretchen's heart, and she cried. She told us later, "I knew right then and there that someday I would be a Mormon. But it wasn't time yet. If I had joined then, it would have been just on emotion. I wanted to make sure that I knew the teachings of the Church for myself."

Back in the United States, Gretchen continued to read and study. When members of her church in Texas found out she was interested in the Mormons, she was attacked on all sides and swamped with anti-Mormon literature. This raised doubts and concerns but none that couldn't be surmounted when the truth was presented.

Several months later, Gretchen flew to Utah for a youth conference at Brigham Young University. As the plane began descending over the Provo area, the sun was setting and the lights of the Provo Temple were shining. Gretchen leaned her head against the window and said, "Heavenly Father, I'm waiting on you." Then came the sweet voice of the Spirit, "Come follow me, Gretchen. It's time."

During the next week, Gretchen completed the missionary discussions. (She said the pictures the missionaries used were much nicer than Brad's airline napkin drawings.) At the end of the week, Gretchen was baptized. Imagine the joy felt by the young people in Japan when word finally reached them. In her home ward in Texas, Gretchen served faithfully despite opposition from friends and family. She then met a wonderful (and handsome) returned missionary, and the next summer, one year after her baptism, they were married in the Salt Lake Temple in Salt Lake City. The elementary school student had passed through high school and college with a solid A grade. It was time now for graduate study.

Gretchen faced great trials to her faith throughout her education in the Church. If she had been relying on her experiences alone, they would not have been enough to see her through when the way got rough. But because she studied hard and found answers on her own, she passed every test and qualifying exam. She had received a testimony of study.

How can parents and leaders help young people find this same level of testimony? It is essential that we teach "true points of doctrine." (Helaman 11:23.) We must teach them clearly to insure comprehension, concretely to ensure a relationship with the real world, and critically enough to invoke self-analysis and inquiry. An excellent time to teach teenagers the doctrinal points of the gospel is in family home evenings. Another good time for teaching is when they are asked to give talks or lessons in church and would like help with their preparation. It is, of course, also appropriate to teach the "true points of doctrine" as a young person asks questions about the gospel or brings up gospel topics in conversation.

"True doctrine, understood, changes attitudes and behavior. The study of the doctrines of the Gospel will improve behavior quicker than a study of behavior will improve behavior," Elder Boyd K. Packer has said. "That is why we stress so forcefully the study of the doctrines of the gospel."

Although the levels of experience and study are testimonies, young people must understand that these alone are not sufficient. We can't make it all the way to the celestial kingdom on half a tank of gas—we need to continue filling the tank.

We all remember the story of the three little pigs. Each built a house for himself, but the pigs who chose to build with straw and sticks were sorry in the long run. The wise pig who built his house of bricks not only provided for his own security but also was able to offer shelter to the other two. When it comes to testimonies, those who build with the straw of experience or the sticks of study alone will not be as safe and happy in the end as those who build with the bricks of revelation. (See Matthew 7:26; 16:18.)

3. Testimony of revelation

The third level of testimony is revelation—when the Spirit bears witness to our spirits. President Joseph Fielding Smith said, "When a man has the manifestation of the Holy Ghost, it leaves an indelible impression on his soul, one that is not easily erased. It is Spirit speaking to spirit, and it comes with convincing force. A manifestation of an angel, or even the Son of God himself, would impress the eye and mind, and eventually become dimmed, but the impressions of the Holy Ghost sink deeper into the soul and are more difficult to erase."

After Barbara and her family were baptized December 12,1981, she still felt that there was a hurdle she had to cross—coming to know without a doubt that The Church of Jesus Christ of Latter-day Saints is the only true church. She had been raised a Catholic and had even lived in a convent for a year in New York City. It was difficult for her to wholeheartedly accept that there could be just one true church.

While she was studying and looking for answers to her question, she was asked to participate in a youth conference in Missouri. After it was over, the stake president invited her and the other speakers to tour some of the Church history sites in the area.

Barbara was so exhausted after the conference that she kept falling asleep during the drive from place to place. When they arrived at Adam-ondi-Ahman, Barbara left the group and started looking for a flower to press in her scriptures for her son on his mission.

"I walked down the hill and bent down to pick a flower," she recalls. "As I stood up, a cloud moved over a large tree nearby. In my mind's eye I thought I saw Christ. He was standing there preaching to a huge crowd—thousands and thousands of people. I got down on my knees, with tears streaming down my cheeks, and whispered over and over again, 'Jesus, I want to be here with you.' As I said these words, I felt that maybe I really *could* be there with him."

When she regained her composure and got back in the car, she asked her companions, "Has anyone ever said anything about Christ being here?"

"Get the book *The Millennial Messiah,* by Elder Bruce R. McConkie," one of the men, a teacher of Church history, said. "It will tell you about Adam-ondi-Ahman."

As soon as Barbara got a chance, she went to an LDS bookstore and found a copy of that book. She was so excited that she sat on the floor right there in the bookstore and opened the book. In it she began reading: Jesus would come to Adam-ondi-Ahman, and He would preach there to tens of thousands of people. It was all written exactly as Barbara had seen it. She knew then, beyond a shadow of a doubt, that this is the one true church. The Lord had given her the testimony of revelation she desired.

At Jesus' death, his apostles were lost. One by one, all became disoriented in the fog, for after two and a half years of being sustained and uplifted by Christ's presence, they were now alone, confused, and discouraged. What changed the doubting, despairing apostles at the crucifixion into the confident, heroic leaders who changed the world? There is but one answer: the revelation that Christ had risen from the grave. Their faith was not based on a dead Savior but on a living one.

That is the same personal revelation we want our young people to ultimately gain. Yet it is something over which we have little control. As parents and leaders, we can't order a spiritual experience for them. We may be able to arrange some of the external elements of experience and study, but that is all we can offer. Personal revelation is an internal process. No wonder President David O. McKay said to Church teachers, "Love the work, do your best, then leave the conversion to the workings of the Spirit of the Lord."

Testimonies of revelation come in the Lord's "own time, and in his own way, and according to his own will." (D&C 88:68.)

One evening after the testimony meeting at an Especially For Youth program on BYU campus, Brad was standing in the doorway of one of the dorms when a young man from California came in, tears streaming down his face, and said, "I know. I know. I have learned for myself."

Brad was struck by what he said because it was almost exactly what Joseph Smith said when he walked out of the grove and into his home in 1820. As Joseph leaned against the fireplace and his mother inquired what the matter was, he replied, "Never mind, all is well—I am well enough off." Then he explained, "I have learned for myself." (Joseph Smith-History 1:20.)

Joseph had received a beautiful testimony of revelation. Yet even *his* essential and world-changing testimony came in levels. Before the grove, there was the groundwork. Before the pillar, there was the prayer. Before the revelation, there was the reading. His internal testimony was built upon a carefully constructed external foundation. His experiences and study had built the faith, humility and obedience necessary for him to receive a perfect knowledge of God's existence.

There are no shortcuts. Advancing from grace to grace— through experience, learning by study and faith, and receiving a fullness of the Holy Ghost—is the way we "grow up" in the things of Christ. (See D&C 93:13; 88:118; Ephesians 4:15.) No one gets to a full tank of gas without passing each measured mark along the way, and no one does that without spending time.

When young people feel that they do not have testimonies, we must help them see that testimonies come in levels. They may already have much more gas in their tank than they realize. We must also remind them that cars don't run forever on a single tank of gas. Testimonies, like gas tanks, must be refilled regularly.

Finally, as parents and leaders, we must realize that our best efforts and offerings are external and secondary to the individual efforts of the youth and the promptings of the Spirit. Testimonies are internal. Each person must nourish his or her testimony "as it beginneth to grow, by . . . faith with great diligence, and with patience, looking forward to the fruit thereof, . . . and behold it shall be a tree springing up unto everlasting life." (Alma 32:41.)

Keys to Action

We can sometimes arrange external conditions our lives, but testimonies are ultimately internal and personal. When teenagers feel that they do not have testimonies, we must help them to understand that testimonies come in levels:

*1. **Experience**, the most basic level at which they will learn for themselves.*

*2. **Study**, which they can undertake with our help as they seek answers to gospel questions, prepare for a talk, or participate in family home evening.*

*3. **Revelation**, which results from the Spirit bearing witness to an individual's spirit an affirmation that the principles of the restored gospel are true.*

CHAPTER 11

Helping Youth Follow the Spirit

The Spirit of God is what ultimately teaches and guides us back to Heavenly Father. We all desire that youth be led more by the Spirit. How can we help them so that they are guided every day? How can we really help them to receive, recognize, and respond to the Spirit?

"There are times when I have been led by something (I know now that it was the Spirit) and have done things I hadn't planned on doing. One day I felt the need to move and live with a distant relative who had offered me a room to stay in. On this whim I took off that very day. A short while later in my new home I was brought the gospel of Jesus Christ by two missionaries. I know that the Spirit inspired me to do what I did. Everyone thought I was crazy to just move like that, but I'm glad I followed the promptings of the Spirit."

When he opened the letter that had just been delivered, Brad felt that it was urgent. "Dear Brother Wilcox," he read. "You probably don't remember me, but I met you last summer at our youth conference. I have since left home and come to college, and I met this really nice guy. As our relationship has grown, he has become more physical. Why not give in to our desires?"

This young woman needed answers—quickly. Since Brad was not her priesthood leader, he wrote and urged her to talk with her bishop. He also quoted from the scriptures and Church leaders reasons why we should remain chaste. After he mailed the letter, he hoped that it would make a difference and that the training she had received in her home would guide her.

Eagerly he opened her reply when it came. "Brother Wilcox, where are you?" he read. "I wrote you because I had a problem, and I didn't know where else to turn. Why haven't you written?" The young lady obviously had not received his letter. Brad panicked, afraid of what he might read next. But no, she had not given in. "I did come very close," she wrote, "but in that moment, I knew it wasn't right, because I wasn't comfortable with the situation. So I got myself out of it."

Brad felt relieved and thankful. She had not needed his letter. She had made the right choice without reading even one of the quotations, examples, or stories. All she needed was what she had been given when she was 8 years old—the gift of the Holy Ghost.

The First Presidency has written in *For the Strength of Youth:* "When you were confirmed a member of the Church, you received the right to the companionship of the Holy Ghost. He can help you make good choices. When challenged or tempted, you do not need to feel alone. The Holy Ghost will help you know right from wrong."

Brad had been trying to guide this young woman, to teach her, to make a difference in her life, without remembering that it is the Spirit who really does those things. The role of parents and leaders is more limited. The offerings of any of us are secondary to the offerings of the Spirit. At best, we can only serve as instruments in God's hands in helping young people learn how to receive, recognize, and respond to the help of the Spirit.

HELPING THEM RECEIVE THE SPIRIT

"You can no more force the Spirit to respond than you can force a bean to sprout, or an egg to hatch before its time," Elder Boyd K. Packer has said. "You can create a climate to foster growth, nourish, and protect, but you cannot force or compel: You must await the growth." The most effective ways to help create a spiritual climate are through prayer, the scriptures, and positive environments.

1. Prayer

Alma the Elder would be the first to remind us that praying for teenagers is not a meaningless ritual or another item on a checklist. (See Mosiah 17:4.) One young man we know has recently experienced a wonderful change of heart about the Church. We have been thrilled as we have watched his attitude, appearance, and entire countenance improve. After he recommitted to full activity in the Church and began earnestly preparing for his mission, his younger sister sent us a short note. Her simple words helped us understand more fully the miracle we had seen happen. "I just wanted to thank you for the time you have spent with my younger brother. Our oldest brother is on his mission in the Philippines. Ever since he left on his mission, he has asked in his prayers that if he were going to receive any blessings for his service in the next two years, that they all be given to his wayward younger brother so he might come back to the truth."

We must *pray* for our youth and *with* our youth. Elder Gene R. Cook, in his book *Raising Up a Family unto the Lord,* shared this story of an experience with a teenage son who had generated some conflict in his family:

"One afternoon a few years ago one of my sons (about 16 at

the time) came home from school very upset about things. He was having trouble learning everything he needed to know for some tests the next day, and some friends had been giving him a hard time as well. He really felt down. In his frustration, he began to cause some contention in the family. My wife and I thought, 'Should we get involved?' As the night wore on, we thought, 'No, we'll let it pass.'"

The next morning, Elder Cook said, "the problems started again at breakfast." After breakfast, he took his son into his bedroom, shut and locked the door, and knelt down. His son, still angry, knelt down also. "I did my best to offer a prayer for him: 'Heavenly Father, bless him. He's hurting today. He's had some problems with the family. He worried about his tests at school' And I expressed my love to him the best I could in that prayer." After a few minutes, Elder Cook's son, humbled, said, "Dad, let me pray." In his prayer he asked for the Lord's forgiveness. Then the father and his son embraced one another, and "the love between the two of them was enriched a hundredfold."

2. Scripture study

In an article in the April 1991 issue of the *Ensign,* Betty Martinsen of Arlington, Texas, described how regular scripture study had touched her family in a way they had not realized. "We thought that our children only tolerated our scripture reading in the morning because I gave them treats if they came on time," she wrote. "But one day, after missing our scripture time for a couple of days, the children were unusually quarrelsome in the car as they came home from school. From the back seat, our 5-year-old piped up, 'We need to start reading the Book of Mormon again, Mom. Everybody is fighting too much.'"

In Helaman 15:7 we learn that study of the scriptures leads directly to faith, repentance, and a change of heart. While Ed J. Pinegar was the president of the Missionary Training Center in Provo, Utah, he focused heavily on teaching missionaries to study scriptures. Once someone asked him why he didn't spend more of his time speaking about other important topics. His answer was simple: "My time with the missionaries is short. If I can get them into the scriptures, then the scriptures will preach to them on every other topic they ever need to hear a sermon on."

3. Positive environments

We can help expose young people to the Spirit when we surround them with things of the Spirit. They must be touched by positive influences, such as family home evenings. We can also encourage expanded friendships and group activities with other young people who are strong in the gospel. We might offer them priesthood blessings, uplifting music, and opportunities for service. We can provide the *New Era* and other youth-oriented Church publications and encourage them to read these materials. We can use pictures of the Savior, prophets, temples, and scripture scenes to create a climate where the Spirit is welcome.

We should strongly urge young people to enroll in seminary and to attend youth conferences and other Church group activities—even if it means dropping another class or having to make special arrangements to get off work. Some professional counselors call this channeling—directing individuals to experiences, friends, and programs that will maintain beliefs and reinforce values taught in the home. Chieko Okazaki has said, "For every child, there is something important about having someone outside the family explain a value held in the family. All parents need partners."

Some may say, "But all they do is sleep through seminary and grump through youth conferences, so what's the use?" Our experience tells us that sleeping students do stir occasionally, and attitudes can change throughout the course of a youth conference. Teenagers stand a better chance of receiving the Spirit in these positive environments than they do while watching TV or playing video games. We have heard many a grateful and tearful testimony begin with the words "I wasn't even going to come, but my parents and leaders talked me into it."

One young woman decided to quit early-morning seminary because she "wasn't getting anything out of it." Her father told her that if nothing else, she was getting one thing—a good habit and routine.

"Oh that's just great," she complained sarcastically.

He explained that such consistency is valuable. Strength comes from frequency and fluency as well as fervency. "Spiritual experiences are like rainstorms in the desert," he said. "You may not know exactly when one will burst upon you, so you just have to be ready all the time. You've got to keep your bucket turned up so that whenever the rain does come, you won't miss it."

According to two LDS scholars, "Youth who experience spirituality rather than just participate in public religious observances are likely to avoid delinquency—even when they live in a hostile environment or have delinquent friends."

HELPING THEM RECOGNIZE THE SPIRIT

In the Book of Mormon, the Savior talked about people who "were baptized with fire and with the Holy Ghost, and they knew it not." (3 Nephi 9:20.) For most of us, the baptism with fire is a continuous process of sanctification. This process may be punctuated now and then by dramatic and sensational events, but usually it comes through a consistently good, right, or peaceful feeling. There are times when the Spirit of God "like a fire is burning." More often, however, it is like a furnace in our homes that is keeping things so warm and comfortable that we don't even think about it unless it breaks down. Adults can help young people learn to recognize the Spirit by helping them to focus on their innermost feelings, taking time to ponder, sharing personal experiences, and testifying of truth.

1. Focusing on their innermost feelings

Seventeen-year-old Krista from Washington said, "Teenagers really do know right from wrong, no matter what we say or do or how much we pretend not to."

When one Latter-day Saint football player turned in his equipment at the end of the high school season, his coach, amid the confusion, counted out an extra dollar of refund money. Out in the hall, the young man—we'll call him Jack—counted the money again. Sure enough, there was an extra dollar.

"So," Brad said, when Jack told him about it later, "I guess you went back into the coach's office and gave it back."

"No," Jack replied. "I put it in my pocket."

"Didn't you feel guilty?"

"No, I felt lucky, like when the phone gives you your quarter back and you think you're receiving blessings for paying your tithing."

"But deep down, didn't you feel guilty?"

"No. It was just a dollar."

"Deep down—really deep down—didn't you feel guilty?"

Finally Jack grudgingly admitted, "Yes. I knew what I should do. But we're not talking about Sunday School here; we're talking real life. The coach already thought I was too much of a goody-goody. What fool would go running back into his office and give the guy the dollar back? Get real!"

The last thing Jack wanted was to look like some kind of religious weirdo to his coach. But still, there were feelings deep inside him that he could not deny.

The following day, Brad learned later, Jack returned the dollar. He did it because the Spirit told him that despite all his rationalization, he was wrong to keep it. And Jack recognized that still, small voice. (Incidentally, he later learned that he had been set up. His coach knew his religious beliefs and deliberately gave him the extra dollar to prove to the assistant coach that Jack wouldn't keep it.)

The First Presidency, in *For the Strength of Youth,* declared, "You cannot do wrong and feel right. It is impossible!"

The delicate and refined communications of the Spirit are not usually seen with our eyes, or heard with our ears. Although the Spirit is often described as a voice, it is usually a voice we feel more than one we hear.

One young woman who wrote to Barbara made the vital association between her feelings and spiritual communication. She said: "I'm a good kid. I'm the vice president on the seminary council this year and class president in Young Women. That is all fine and good, but I had a strange feeling deep down that I was kind of just going through the motions and playing a part for other people. I knew the Spirit was telling me I should be more sincere. This past week I got back in touch with myself and with the Lord. I feel so good now. I feel like a new person."

2. Taking time to ponder

"The things of God are of deep import," Joseph Smith said, "and time, and experience, and careful and ponderous and solemn thoughts can only find them out." Pondering is serious reflection, an attitude of spiritual searching that is consistently the seedbed of revelation. This is why our friend Randal A. Wright tells teenagers, "Use quiet times. One thing we must learn about the Holy Ghost is that he whispers his messages to us. We live in a fast-paced, noisy society. From the moment most teenagers get up in the morning until they go to bed at night there is almost nonstop noise. What with radio, television, movies, video games, and so on, little time is left for listening to the Spirit. One of the most rewarding things we can do is to spend some quiet time and just listen to what the Spirit whispers to us. . . . You will be amazed at the insights that will be revealed."

We as parents and leaders understand this, but how can we teach the importance of this principle to teens? We can't always keep the stereo from playing and the phone from ringing, and yet young people can and must learn how to take quiet moments to listen to the Spirit of the Lord. The importance of pondering can be seen in how we should quietly listen to the Lord as we say our prayers as well as speak to him. Family home evening lessons are a good time to teach this topic.

In the Book of Mormon, Amulek admitted, "I was called many times and I would not hear." (Alma 10:6.) As with this servant of God, our young people are also called regularly by the Spirit. Often, it is not wickedness or sin that keeps them from hearing the Spirit. Rather, they are preoccupied and involved with so many things that they are not taking time to listen, ponder, and reflect upon matters of significance.

3. Sharing personal experiences

Michele, a 14-year-old girl from Idaho, said she wished parents would "share special moments and memories with teenagers. That is the best thing you can do for us." Nothing reaches and teaches more effectively than personal experience. As we honestly share our memories, feelings, struggles, and growth experiences with young people, they can relate to us, and the lessons we are teaching become more meaningful.

You may be thinking, "But nothing dramatic or exciting has ever happened to me," or "I'm not an expert or authority." The fact that we have gone through teenage years ourselves and lived to tell about it makes us all experts to a degree. Our lives, however uneventful they may seem to us, are excellent resources that we can use when we teach young people. Our experiences can help them to see how values and standards apply to the real world and how they can use these same values and standards in their own lives.

Barbara remembers her first youth conference assignment. She stood in front of the youth with great decorum and said sweetly, "Take out your scriptures, class, and turn to Proverbs, chapter three, verses five and six." They tuned her out after one glance, and she did nothing to change their minds. To those teenagers on that day, Barbara was, in her own words, "a living sleeping pill."

As the weekend drew to a close, she shared her dismay with Brad. Through clenched teeth she said, "This is my first youth conference and my last. I'll never do this again. I mean it!" "Barbara, don't look at it like that," Brad responded. "Try to remember back to when you were their age. Think of experiences in your own early life that youth can relate to." Barbara now says, "That was some of the best advice I ever received." She began telling the youth about when the scriptures became important to her and how she felt at her baptism and as a new convert in the Church. She shares the lessons she learned from a painful past and how the Spirit has guided her in making important decisions. Now the young people who hear her do not sleep or think to themselves, "This lady has no clue how I feel." Instead, they respond as if they have found a personal friend who understands exactly what they are going through.

4. Testifying of truth

We must bear our testimonies often—and not just in church meetings. When we do this, we offer young people a support upon which they can lean until they are ready to stand alone. It is true that one cannot live on borrowed light, but sometimes it is only in the glow of borrowed light that we see clearly enough to kindle our own lamps.

One young missionary recalled: "My dad always told us how much he loved the Savior and the Church. In fact, he told us of his love for the Book of Mormon and the living prophets so often that my family sometimes teased him about it." But then the young man was away from home for a few days and felt discouraged and disoriented. "My father's testimony came back to my mind over and over," he recalled. "I felt the Spirit, and I knew that if my dad could know these things with such surety, then so could I."

We all need to be more direct in teaching young people to recognize the Spirit. They must understand that the Spirit doesn't come from having a testimony meeting in the mountains or on a beach. It doesn't come from soft lights or atmosphere. It doesn't come from speaking dramatically or from crying, although tears are often associated with the tender feelings of the Spirit. The Spirit confirms truth. When we share our most sincere feelings about

Christ, the Church, and things of eternal significance, then we have spoken truth and the Spirit will come.

HELPING THEM RESPOND TO THE SPIRIT

Because agency is one of our God-given gifts, each individual must choose whether or not to respond to promptings of the Spirit. However, we can help young people make the right choice if we express love and clear expectations to them, show them we care, challenge them, and are prepared to hear the Spirit's direction ourselves.

1. Expressing love and clear expectations

Our love and expectations must be stated clearly to young people. As parents and leaders, we would do well to follow the example of the First Presidency, who wrote to the youth, "We want you to know that we love you. We have great confidence in you. Because of that, we talk to you frankly and honestly."

Sometimes parents and leaders assume that they are showing love by lowering standards for young people. This is a fallacy. The Spirit can be with us only when we are striving to keep our covenants and live the principles of the gospel. Whether it means not letting teens enter a stake dance when we know they have been drinking or not allowing them to date before they're 16, we must not be afraid of taking stands on standards.

Barbara sometimes hears parents say, "Let him make up his own mind," or "We shouldn't impose our will on her." When it comes to choices with eternal significance, aren't these statements rationalizations for weaknesses in our own convictions? Research by professional counselors has concluded that religions or family settings that present teenagers with clearly defined values and then freedom to choose for themselves are most successful in helping to develop mature faith in the lives of their young people.

Brad remembers once when he declared to his father, "I'm not going to church this Sunday. I have my free agency, and I don't have to go if I don't want to."

His dad only shrugged and said, "All right. But since you'll have so much extra time this morning, the workroom downstairs needs a thorough cleaning."

Brad thought of the piles of sawdust, scrap wood, and paint cans in the workroom. "You're not being fair," he snapped. "You just want me to go to church."

"You're right," his father said, "but you have your free agency. Will it be church or the workroom?" With those options to choose from, Brad quickly grabbed his coat and tie, and he has been grabbing them gratefully ever since.

The parent who would do anything necessary to save a drowning child at the local swimming pool wouldn't give a thought as to whether that's what the child might want. A loving parent wouldn't lose a single stroke while wondering if he were imposing on a son or daughter's free agency to drown. Is the same parent then going to sit helplessly by and sigh, "It's her life" or "How do I know what's best for him?" when a daughter begins dating too early or a son begins renting R-rated videos?

Elder Boyd K. Packer has stated, "I do not appeal for the lowering of standards. Just the opposite. More lost sheep will respond quicker to high standards than they will to low ones." Then he adds, "Spiritual discipline framed in love and confirmed with testimony will help redeem souls."

2. Showing them we care

One young woman told about a time in her life when, she said, "I wanted to make my own decisions and not just do everything because I'm my parents' daughter. So I really let loose."

One night she came home from being with her friends and doing some things that she knew were wrong. "My father looked me right in the eyes, and I knew he wasn't thinking, 'Can't you see what you are doing to *me?*' It was more like 'Can't you see what you are doing to *you?*' That's all I could think about the whole week. I knew I was making my parents unhappy, but now I realize I was making myself unhappy too. I was trying to live one way when I really knew another way was right." Her father's sincere love and care made a difference and were more effective than any lecture he could have offered.

3. Challenging them

Young people are capable of rising to spiritual challenges. For a youth conference one year, the stake leaders took the young people to an amusement park and lodged them in a luxury hotel. The next year they tried a different type of activity. Following the counsel of church leaders, they decided to take the focus off joy rides at an amusement park and put it on true joy by planning spiritual workshops and a service project for the young people.

At first the teenagers weren't very excited about the change, but as the conference progressed, they began to see things in a new light. The testimony meeting at the end of the youth conference was far different from the one a year earlier when, one of the leaders said, "Most of the youth just sat and giggled and poked each other." But this time, the young people were eager to express their joy at having served others and their love for Jesus Christ.

4. Being prepared to hear

As parents and leaders, we have many ways available to us as we try to help young people learn to rely on the Holy Ghost. But perhaps the best way is knowing the voice of the Spirit very well for ourselves. When we are dedicated and worthy, the Spirit will guide us in our efforts.

"I knew it wasn't right because I wasn't comfortable," the young woman mentioned at the beginning of this chapter wrote in her letter to Brad. When temptation came, no other source of help could have been so effective as the voice of the Spirit. She was able to receive it, recognize it, and respond properly. As teenagers gain this kind of spiritual ability, they will soon discover on their own that there are far fewer things they can do in the world and still retain the guidance and influence of the Spirit. But instead of feeling restricted, they will begin to sense the liberating power of Christ and finally understand what real freedom is.

Keys to Action

Parents and leaders can really help youth to receive, recognize, and respond to the Spirit by implementing the following suggestions.

*1. **Receiving the Spirit:** The most effective ways to help create a spiritual climate come through prayer, scripture study, and positive environments.*

*2. **Recognizing the Spirit:** We can teach youth how to recognize the Spirit by helping them to focus on their innermost feelings, taking time to ponder, sharing personal experiences, and testifying of truth.*

*3. **Responding to the Spirit:** Young people can learn how to make good choices if we express our love and make our expectations clear, challenge them, and prepare to hear the Spirit's direction.*

PART TWO

Guiding Priniciples
That Really Help

CHAPTER 12

Broadening Your View

Beliefs drive behavior. In working with young people, we must try to stretch our vision and see the grandeur of the spirits in our charge. We must see them as they are now, but also as they can be in the future. In viewing youth, how can we shift from telephoto to wide-angle lenses?

"I get so many mixed messages in my life—my seminary teacher tells me I'm special, but my coach calls me lazy and good-for-nothing and a few other things I don't like to repeat. My mom is a member of the Church and tries hard to live the gospel, but my stepfather is not a member and is not supportive. He is really intellectual, and he laughs at a lot of the teachings of the Church. My mom tells me I'll be a good missionary, but my stepfather says that I'm stupid to even consider wasting two years on a mission when I should be in school. He says that I'm only proving my ignorance by clinging to the Church, and that I should have outgrown my need for religion a long time ago."

When Brad was a small boy, his family visited the pyramids in Egypt. As they approached the famous monuments, his parents were amazed at the sight. His older brothers were fascinated. But Brad couldn't see what all the fuss was about. He thought the hotel where the family was staying was a lot nicer than these big old dusty things.

How the members of Brad's family perceived the Egyptian pyramids made a big difference in how they valued them and acted
toward them. The same is true with teenagers. Will we see our
young people as the wonders of the world or simply wonder what
in the world we are going to do with them?

Brad's parents-in-law served as missionaries on Temple Square
in Salt Lake City. As they met thousands of visitors from all over
the world, they encountered a range of different opinions about
the Church. One gentleman had never heard of the Church prior
to taking their tour but later told them, "I have felt the Spirit of
God in this special place. Your church is the best thing to ever happen to the world. How do I learn more?"

Compare that experience with another occasion when many
young people of a different faith were bused into Salt Lake City and
surrounded Temple Square, carrying picket signs and chanting
loudly. Brad's father-in-law and other missionaries approached
them and invited them to come take a tour or see a video. The missionaries were treated only with disrespect. Finally Brad's father-in-
law approached one of the leaders of the group and asked, "What is
it that you want here?" The leader said, "We are praying for the
spirit of Satanism to leave this place."

Beliefs drive behavior. The actions of this man who was fighting against the Church, and the actions of the humble visitor who
later joined the Church, both began with the point-of-view from
which they chose to look at Temple Square.

In working with young people, we must try to stretch our
vision and see the grandeur of the spirits in our charge. We must
remember the eternal potential of these young people regardless of
their current choices. We must see our own efforts in working with
the youth as being worthwhile even when we see no immediate

outward evidence of their effectiveness. In viewing youth, perhaps more of us need to shift from telephoto to wide-angle lenses.

1. See greatness

Barbara's husband, Hal, once showed us a sign he thought should be posted on every teenager's bedroom door. It said, "Tired of being harassed by your stupid parents? Act now! Move out, get a job, pay your own bills while you still know everything."

Teenagers can try us to the limits and exasperate us. One mother said, "My son makes me so mad that I'd like to use him for a pinata at the next ward party!" But then there are other moments—those shining Camelot moments when everything goes right and our hope is restored.

One such Camelot moment came for Brad when he was mingling with some teenagers before giving a talk. He asked a young man, "How old are you?"

The boy replied, "I'm almost 16."

Brad teased him a little, asking, "What are you most excited for, the dating or the driving?"

The young man's response was unexpected. "The thing I'm most excited for is that now I can baptize my friend."

Young people are worth our every effort. They are worth our time and trouble. They are worth everything we can do. On Brad's office wall, right behind his desk, is a picture of Helaman's warriors, a favorite since he was young. It used to simply remind him of the beautiful and inspiring Book of Mormon story it depicts. However, these days when he looks at it, he doesn't see only valiant young people who stood for truth centuries ago. Now he sees the faces of young people he meets throughout the Church. He sees the strength and firm positive direction of these wonderful spirits who are not only beloved by God but also entrusted by Him with great responsibilities. He feels love for the youth.

In Alma 36 we read of a wonderful conversation between Alma and his son Helaman. Alma thanks his son for being such a great young man, so much stronger than Alma was as a youth. Our friend Scott Anderson tells of reading this scripture one day and realizing that he had a great son too. "He was definitely better than I had ever been at his age," Scott says. "It occurred to me that I had seldom expressed that idea to him. When I got home that night, I called him into my study. We sat down to have a man-to-man talk. I tried to be like Alma and thank him for his great example, and then I said, 'I think you must have been my big brother in heaven.' He agreed with me and exclaimed, 'Dad, I've been thinking the same thing!'"

Chieko Okazaki has written, "When we learn that 'it is only with the heart that one can see rightly, we develop spiritual eyes to look upon the inward person. When we do this, we will discover a wonderful secret: Every person is, as it were, the Savior in disguise. In every person, we will see the divine son or daughter of God for whom Jesus Christ suffered and died. And with such a view, how can we help loving each other?"

After a youth dance, several leaders stayed to clean up. Two of them were complaining about the struggles they were having with some of the young people in their wards. One said, "I'm sick of hearing how special these young people are. If they are that special, why don't they act like it?" The other said, "I know. The youth seem to take the Church so lightly—not like when we were growing up."

The bishop, folding chairs nearby, overheard their conversation and realized that perhaps they needed a broader view. The following Sunday he handed them a copy of an address Elder Boyd K. Packer once gave to the youth. Elder Packer said:

"I wish we could promise you that the world will be safer and easier for you than it was for us. But we cannot make that promise, for just the opposite is true. There are temptations beckoning to you that were not there when we were teenagers. AIDS had not been invented when we were young, and drugs were something a doctor prescribed. We knew about opium from reading mysteries, but steroids, pills, and crack and all the rest belonged to future imaginations. Modesty was not mocked then. Morality and courtesy were fostered in books and films as much as their opposites are today. Perversion was not talked about, much less endorsed as a life-style. What was shunned then as pornographic you see now on prime time television. Your challenge is *much* greater than was ours. Few of us would trade places with you. Frankly, we are quite relieved that we are not back where you are. Few of us would be equal to it."

2. See potential

Jay was a handsome young man, strong, athletic, and popular. Some people in his ward said that he was a young man who had everything going for him. But Jay's father, who knew his son better than others did, recognized many weaknesses along with the strengths. He said, "I finally had to disconnect the phone in the house because he simply would not stop placing long-distance calls to all the girls he would meet around the state at athletic events. He was costing me a fortune."

The father was also concerned at Jay's lack of attention to schoolwork and his attitude that he could get by well enough without giving his best effort. Their relationship suffered. Jay's father was putting up with Jay more than he was enjoying him. It was almost as if he had said to himself, "Just a few more years and he'll be gone. I'll just endure till then."

Then a guest speaker came to Jay's early-morning seminary class. He spoke about how each young person was saved to come forth in these latter days and how each one had a unique mission to perform. The speaker challenged each of the students to prepare themselves to receive their patriarchal blessings. The Spirit touched Jay deeply.

"I want to prepare to receive my patriarchal blessing," he told his parents. They were surprised. His father thought that this spurt of enthusiasm would soon fade as it had in the past with other plans and goals. However, Jay's enthusiasm endured. He contacted the bishop himself to ask for an interview.

The day of the blessing arrived. This was not a new experience for Jay's parents. They had sat through several other blessings with their older children. But shortly after the patriarch began giving the blessing, Jay's father was astonished. He listened to incredible words being uttered and blessings promised. He thought, "Is the patriarch talking about *my* son?" He heard of wonderful things that were in store for his son—the powerful influence this boy would be for good in his family, in the Church, and in the world.

When they arrived home, he sought out his son, and together they recalled the powerful blessing just received. He promised, "Things are going to change around here. We're going to start holding family prayer and family home evening again. We're going to start our family scripture study again too. I'm going to do all I can to make this home a better training camp for you."

Jay's father now saw his son through different eyes. During the following year whenever he felt frustrated with Jay's immaturity, he would reread the patriarchal blessing and focus on his son's great potential.

Working with teenagers is a lot like opening presents at Christmas; the fact that the packages are wrapped makes the experience all the better. Christmastime might be easier if everyone knew right up front what was in each box. There would be a lot less exchanging and guessing. By the same token, there would be a lot less joy. The possibilities, with all their surprises, make Christmas exciting and even enriching. When we are dealing with teenagers, we must remember that many of their greatest gifts are still wrapped inside, waiting to be discovered.

In order to know and love teenagers, teachers and leaders usually must begin working with them long before they have grown. After a year or two, a leader can look at the loud and cocky Kurt, yet still see the vulnerability inside. Then it is more tolerable to be with him. Once the teacher finds that quiet Stephanie has a great deal to say when people listen, once the teacher becomes proud of Maria's feistiness and desire to learn, it's easier to work with them. But in the beginning, when Kurt just seems loud, Stephanie withdrawn, and Maria full of questions that are always off the subject, it's difficult to be patient. During times when it seems hard to put up with teenagers, look through a wide-angle lens. See them as they are now, but also as they can be in the future.

3. See your efforts as worthwhile

Brad attended a youth conference where one of the adult leaders brought a book to finish reading. During all the workshops, service projects, and dances, he sat off to the side and read. Later he was encouraged to get involved with the youth, and he discovered the difference between giving his time and sharing himself.

At the conference testimony meeting the leader stood up and said in honesty, "I used to make up excuses to not be with young people because I felt awkward and unsure around them. But at this conference you have shown me that I do have something to offer. Now I'm going to start making excuses to be with you instead of the other way around."

Righteous and sincere efforts with the youth are never wasted. Whether our impact is recognized immediately or not, it is felt. Young people live better lives when we share what is uniquely ours to offer. We must not underestimate the impact of a smile, a touch, a compliment, a funny joke, a shoulder to cry on, or a listening ear, all of which have the potential of turning a life around. "Cast your bread upon the water," the saying goes, "and it will come back to you." However, it may not always come back according to our timetable.

One young man was preparing for his mission. He was busily shopping for suits and white shirts. He was filling out forms and setting appointments for exams with his doctor and dentist. One afternoon he was cleaning out his bedroom (much to the delight of his eager little brother), and the young man found some papers and reports he had saved from elementary school. He smiled as he remembered the fun he had had and the positive influence his teachers had been in his life. He thought, "I wonder if they even know how much they helped me." That same day, he wrote to some of his favorite teachers to say thanks and to let them know about his mission call.

A few days before he entered the Missionary Training Center, a letter came from his second grade teacher. "You will never know how much your note meant to me," she wrote. "In all my years of teaching I have rarely received such a wonderful uplift. I cried to think that anything I said and did those many years ago may have helped you. It is easy to become discouraged in this profession, wondering if you are making any difference at all. You made my day, my week, my year! God bless you on your mission."

At those times when life begins to seem like a never-ending string of lessons no one listens to, family night activities no one cares about, meals no one appreciates, and written letters and notes no one acknowledges, we must switch to wide-angle lenses and broaden our view.

How many parents, teachers, and leaders sacrifice time and talents only to be cruelly judged and criticized? Why do bishops and stake presidents serve complainers? Why do missionaries labor to help those they don't even know? Why? To serve a God they do know.

"When ye are in the service of your fellow beings ye are only in the service of your God." (Mosiah 2:17.) A crying baby in the middle of the night or a misbehaving child at school may need the most love at the very moment when they are least loveable. By broadening our view, we can continue to work with even the most difficult of teenagers out of compassion—if not for the teenager at the moment, then certainly for the Savior, who said, "Inasmuch as ye have done it unto the least of these . . . ye have done it unto me." (Matthew 25:40.)

At the end of our lives we won't remember the cars we drove or the awards we received as much as we will remember the time we spent with family and friends. We will remember the efforts we made to help, lift, and love others. We will have earned our treasures in heaven by treasuring heavenly things.

Imagine a tourist looking at the Pyramids of Egypt, the Great Wall of China, or the Grand Canyon through only a telephoto lens. Think of all he would miss. To enjoy the broader beauty and significance of these wonders of the world, a wide-angle lens is required.

The same is true with teenagers. As we see greatness, potential, and the worth of our own efforts, then we have broadened our view with wide-angle lenses that allows us to see young people as the true wonders they are and will be.

CHAPTER 13

All You Can Do

Sometimes all we can do is still not enough. Children sometimes make unwise choices, and at those times perhaps we can only pray for them, have faith in their ability to change, keep loving them, and hang on. But we can't get down on ourselves.

"As I think back to a few years ago when I left home and left the Church and was going my own way, I know that I caused my parents a great deal of grief. They worried about me, but at the time I was simply determined to do things my way, and nothing was going to stop me. Now things are better. I've had a lot of repenting to do, and there have been lots of tears. I want my parents to know that the choices I made when I was younger don't mean that they were bad parents. I just needed to learn some things on my own."

A pastor in a Protestant church sat at his desk preparing a sermon. He was going to speak at a funeral service. This task was nothing new. In fact, he had made similar preparations so many times before that he already had a filing cabinet full of appropriate comments and thoughts. But this time was different. He struggled, even agonized over what he should say. This time the sermon was for the funeral of his own son, who had committed suicide a few days earlier.

Most people in the congregation had noticed how rebellious the boy had become. Most of them had also seen the pain it was causing this good father. Still, no one was too worried about the situation. After all, the pastor was a wonderful father, and the son had a moral and religious upbringing. Things would work out all right in the end, so they thought. But the end had now come much sooner than anyone expected, and things hadn't worked out at all.

The pastor looked at the blank papers before him and began to cry. He felt sure there were no more tears to fall. Hadn't he used them all up in the last few days? Yet once again they came flooding down his cheeks. No one would ever know the sorrow that filled him. The guilt and failure he felt were profound.

Just then there was a slight tap at the office door. The pastor sat up and wiped his eyes with the back of his hand. "Come in," he called. A woman in his congregation entered the room. She was helping to make some of the funeral arrangements, but upon seeing the pastor, she knew it wasn't a good time. She turned to leave. He said, "Please don't go. I don't want to be alone right now."

She wondered what to say. It seemed all the regular words, such as "I'm so sorry," and "Time heals all wounds," had already been said too many times by too many people. Quietly the woman said, "I don't know much about these sorts of things, but I do know that sometimes all you can do is still not enough."

The pastor said nothing. The woman left the room but her words lingered: "Sometimes all you can do is still not enough." Strangely, those words brought the first comfort the pastor had felt for days. He and his wife were only human. All they could do as parents was to try their best, and if this was one of those times when their best was still not enough, then the matter was in God's hands. The pastor turned back to his papers and began to write his sermon, "Sometimes all you can do is still not enough. . . ."

A mother wrote to Brad from Japan, where her family lived because of a military assignment. Her letter was not legible in places because her tears had blurred the ink. She and her husband were doing all in their power to help their struggling teens, and still the teens were making poor choices.

All Brad could write in response was, "Hang in and hang on." He told her that while we are all aware that no other success can compensate for failure in the home, as President David 0. McKay taught, we must also remember that sometimes even the greatest diligence in doing our part is insufficient—at least temporarily against the effects of others' agency. Children sometimes make unwise choices, and at those times, perhaps we can only pray for them, have faith in their ability to change, keep loving them, and hang on. But we can't get down on ourselves.

One sister approached us after a class we taught. Her heart was broken. She said, "I don't even know why I came. I just feel so full of guilt."

"What's wrong?" Barbara asked.

"A few months ago my son was sent home from his mission dishonorably. He has been excommunicated and remains totally unrepentant and bitter." She started to cry. "I've done all I can. So has his father," she explained through her sobs.

"Then you have no reason to feel guilty," Barbara said. "Your boy does, but you don't."

"But I must have done something wrong somewhere along the line, or things would never have turned out like this."

Later we received a letter from this sister. She was still full of grief. "I have given and given of myself to that kid," she wrote.

"I've gone so many extra miles for him, I could never count them all. It's not fair that boys from negative and abusive homes can stay close to the Church and serve honorable missions with no support from parents, while my husband and I hold regular home evenings, scripture study, and family prayers, and our boy blows it." She felt humiliated and embarrassed. She wrote about going to her bishop and asking to be released from her calling in Primary. When he asked her why, she said, "I can't bring up my own kid right. I don't think other parents will want me messing with their kids." She wouldn't raise her hand or offer any comments in Sunday classes because she felt that she had nothing worthwhile to say. She wrote, "I just don't feel like I can teach a lesson, give advice, or be an example to anyone."

We wrote back and suggested that this sister talk to her priesthood leaders about what she was feeling. We must never forget that we cannot control another's agency. It was the young man himself who had chosen to do wrong. Perhaps he rationalized about it, trying to justify his actions. Perhaps he was blaming others or even pretending that what he did really wasn't wrong or that he "didn't know any better." But he is accountable for his own actions. Mercifully, the gospel provides a way for people to see things clearly, choose the right, and overcome misbehavior if they so choose. We can continually try to teach and persuade them in love, but then we have done our part.

Conversion, reactivation, friendshipping, fellowshipping, or any influence we can have upon others—including our own children-depends upon three parts. God will always do his part. We must do our part, and the others must do theirs. It's much like a stool that depends upon three legs. If one leg happens to give way when someone sits on the stool, is it the fault of the two legs that stood strong?

We often hear the statement of President Harold B. Lee, "The greatest work you will do will be within the walls of your home," without remembering that within those walls, parents are not the only ones with responsibilities. The word *you* refers just as much to children and teenagers as to parents. For this reason, the measure of our success as parents will never rest solely on how our children turn out. Elder Boyd K. Packer explained, "That judgment would be just only if we could raise our families in a perfectly moral environment, and that now is not possible."

Sometimes we as parents and leaders condemn ourselves if the teenagers that we love go astray. We must not forget the important principle of forgiveness. If we choose not to follow our prophet leaders, is it a reflection on our prophets' worthiness or diligence? Of course not. Just because the people of Noah's day did not follow him does not mean that Noah missed the boat. In a world of free agents, where there are knowledge, accountability, opportunity, ability, and responsibility, choices ultimately rest squarely on the shoulders of those who make them.

The mother of the boy who was sent home from his mission later wrote us another letter. She said: "Things are going better. My husband and I talked to our bishop, and we are slowly learning how to choose happiness independent of the actions or attitudes of anyone—else-including our son. It will be hard to erase the hurt, and there are still feelings of guilt, but we decided we must face this challenge with perspective and the quiet confidence borne of the Spirit."

At the bottom of the letter was this addition: "P.S. The bishop asked me to speak in sacrament meeting, and I accepted. I'm also teaching Primary again. I gave a lesson about Abinadi, and I'm feeling especially close to him these days. I too have things to say that are worthwhile, whether anyone listens and follows or not."

Our friend Curt Galke told us of an experience that happened to him when he was training to be a doctor. As part of his residency, he was working in a hospital emergency room when several teenagers who had been in a knife fight were brought in. Curt was assigned to work on a boy who appeared to be about 15. There were two or three stab wounds that would need to be closed, but the one that worried Curt the most was a small puncture wound on the left side of the boy's chest. Suddenly the boy's pulse dropped, and there were dangerous changes in his blood pressure. Curt and the emergency room doctor he was working with concluded that a knife must have penetrated the boy's heart and left a hole that was bleeding.

Curt says, "The doctor moved quickly. Making sure the boy was adequately sedated, he took a scalpel and made an incision from the breastbone around to the boy's back. He spread the patient's ribs apart and asked me to reach into the chest and pull his heart to the surface so we could examine it. I did as I was asked. I couldn't believe it. I actually had a young man's heart beating in my hand."

Curt and the doctor found the hole and repaired it. You would think that the youth would never have survived such an ordeal, but he did. Curt stayed with him until he awoke in intensive care. Curt imagined his first words would be, "Gee, thanks," or "My chest hurts!" Instead, the boys first words were "Did I get him? Do you know if I killed the other guy?" Curt realized then that medical skill may have been able to repair a heart, but it could not change a heart. All we can do is our part. The rest is up to God and the other person.

If all of us were perfect parents and leaders living in a perfect world, none of this would be a concern. But we're not perfect, and we're certainly not in a perfect world. One mother said, "I wish I had known earlier what I know now. There is nothing like raising children to make you feel like a bumbling child yourself." All we can do is sincerely give it our best shot. President Brigham Young said," 'Be ye as perfect as ye can,' for that is all we can do. . . . When we are doing as well as we know how in the sphere and station that we occupy here, we are justified."

Our children's teenage years usually hit us when we are the most pressured at work, rearing younger children, paying the most bills, and worrying about our own aging parents. It's okay to have highs and lows, and everything we say does not have to sound as if it is straight out of a Church commercial. Mistakes are allowed for both children and adults. They are part of learning and growing for everyone.

The fact is, when young people see us stumble along at times and realize that we are not all-knowing, perfect parents and leaders, it often helps them to relate better to us. When we have "one of those days," it can help us feel more understanding and empathetic toward our teenagers. Mutual vulnerability can sometimes bring us closer.

One father was beside himself as he saw his bright and handsome son "throw it all away." The boy didn't want to finish working on his Eagle, go to school, or commit to a mission. He gave up seminary and church activity. His bishop and leaders tried to talk to him, but they were met with cold stares. The father felt frustrated, "That boy has more talent and ability in his little finger than I do in my whole body. But I can't do it for him. I'm afraid he will have to learn a few lessons the hard way."

The father knew that his son might have been able to drop out of scouting, school, and seminary, but he could not drop out of learning. All the boy had really managed to do was to select more difficult courses from the hardest teachers of all: experience and pain. These teachers give the test first and the lessons later. It is said that such a school is for fools, but we can understand when students enroll there. Haven't we all been through just such a class or two ourselves? Research studies claim that making painful mistakes is usually what motivates us to finally start thinking things through before we act. Such mistakes help us develop problem-solving skills. Some experts claim that some rebellion or disillusionment can even be healthy and necessary for growth, maturity, and internalized values.

At the end of a class we taught at Education Week, we expressed some of the ideas we have shared in this chapter. Soon after we received a letter from a concerned mother. She wrote: "When I attended your class, my heart was literally breaking over the relationship my husband and I had with our daughter. Hardly a day would go by that I wasn't dissolved to tears over her hatred of me, our family, school, church, etc. Somewhere I lost my little girl. You said, 'Hang in there. You are only responsible for your part. You cannot do your teenager's part, and you cannot do God's part.' That was when I finally felt my most desperate prayers answered. I was able to let go of some of the guilt I didn't deserve. I felt comforted when you said, 'Does Heavenly Father feel guilty when his children make poor choices? He may feel sorrow and great sadness but not guilt. We're not alone in our parental concerns. God will be there. They are His kids too.'"

In his book *The Mount and the Master,* Elder Robert E. Wells of the Seventy said, "The saying 'You can lead a horse to water but you cannot make him drink' is valid indeed. You can expose people to all sorts of spiritual experiences or scriptures or situations, but unless they have a deep desire or appetite that needs to be satisfied within themselves, it is all to no avail . . . Unless we want to come unto Christ, no one can push us there."

In Mormon 3:16, Mormon characterizes himself as an idle witness—not that he was indolent or inactive in doing his part. Another meaning of the word *idle* is "unused." Though Mormon's warnings and preachings were left idle—unused—by his people, he still stood as a witness. We too must stand as witnesses to our children, love them unconditionally, and be ready, with open arms, at all times to welcome them back.

CHAPTER 14

The Light Guiding Them Home

Inside every person is a divine spirit that will recall and respond to eternal light and truth. We cannot underestimate how personally involved Heavenly Father is in the lives of his children—and that includes the turbulent lives of his teenagers. We are not alone in our parental concerns.

"What is my message to parents and leaders? I am dreadfully sorry for the heartache and worry I have caused you. Thanks for your unconditional love and support through everything. That love and support have meant the most."

Many young men like to carry pictures of beautiful girls in their wallets to impress their friends. When they pull out their wallets to get some money, they thumb through the pictures so that any onlooker will know how many females there are in the world who would die without them.

Brad remembers in high school when the picture of a new girl showed up in the wallet of his friend Steven Kapp Perry. "Wow! Who is that?" Brad asked, examining the picture closely.

"Believe it or not, it's my cousin," Steve bragged. "We had a family get-together over the weekend, and she gave me that picture."

Brad spent the next week trying to figure out a way to be

invited to the next family get-together. The cousin in the picture in Steve's wallet really was beautiful. She and Steve were around the same age and felt especially close to each other. Like Steve, she also had wonderful parents and a loving family. They were all strong in the gospel.

Then things started to change. It wasn't anything that happened overnight—just small things that slowly turned into big things, and big things that soon became huge things. Throughout high school, the new pictures Steve would show Brad of his cousin were different somehow. She was still beautiful. It was just that her countenance was changed.

In the years that followed, the girl ultimately left the Church. Her choice hurt the family deeply. She gave up the Church to join a polygamist group.

Steve, like everyone else in the family, felt a tremendous loss. He struggled with his cousin's decision and felt personally hurt and rejected. He missed her—not just her presence at the traditional get-togethers, but also how she used to be. He missed the girl who was once in his wallet. He said, "I kept thinking of the grief her parents were feeling. I thought about my own pain and wanted so much to do something—anything. I guess helplessness is the worst feeling of all. But I knew that there was one thing I could do, no matter what. I could show my faith by still loving her." Later he wrote this song, dedicated to his cousin:

> The road that you walk is so different from mine.
> And things we believed you have left far behind.
> You're turning from things that are tender to me
> To follow a star that I never can see.
> In all of your searching for answers and ends,

Did you ever consider the place you began?
For the table is set and there's bread to be broken,
Sweet words of forgiveness to be spoken all around.
And there's living water to quench all your thirsting.
And maybe the end of all your searching will be found.
As day follows day I have started to see
That love does not mean we will always agree.
I cannot pretend that I know how you feel.
All that I know is that I love you still.
No matter what roads you've traveled alone,
I just hope you know you can always come home.
So I'll set my love like a candle in the window
That someday in the distance you may see the light
And come home.

Few things are as warm and inviting as a candle in the window. However, when nights are cold and the window frosts over, it's easy to become discouraged and wonder if our little light will even be seen. It's easy to lose hope. But if we will keep the candle in place, then the heat of the flame will slowly melt a small circle in the frost. Our light will shine through into the darkness. And then, like Steve, we can hope that maybe someday the ones we pray for will see the light and come home. There is a Spanish saying that, when translated, says, "The most wonderful thing about happy endings is that sometimes they happen."

No matter how far away our young people may appear at times, inside every person is a divine spirit that will recall and respond to eternal light and truth. We are told that those who "confess not his hand in all things" can offend God. (D&C 59:21.) We cannot underestimate how personally involved Heavenly

Father is in the lives of his children—and that includes the turbulent lives of his teenagers. We are not alone in our parental concerns.

Barbara knows of one couple, faithful Latter-day Saint parents, who lost one of their children for a time to influences over which they had no control. Their hearts were broken. They suffered and agonized over their child's rebelliousness. They felt both guilt and grief. Some who were close to the situation were puzzled and said things like, "And after these parents have been so loyal to the Church and kept all the commandments, why would this happen? After that child was reared in the gospel, how could she stray so far from its precepts?"

This couple found that a positive change in their feelings and their ability to go on occurred when they read a statement made in general conference in April 1929 by Elder Orson F. Whitney: "The Prophet Joseph Smith declared—and he never taught a more comforting doctrine—that the eternal sealings of faithful parents and the divine promises made to them for valiant service in the Cause of Truth, would save not only themselves, but likewise their posterity. Though some of the sheep may wander, the eye of the Shepherd is upon them, and sooner or later . . . either in this life or the life to come, they will return."

In his book *Charity Never Faileth,* Elder Vaughn J. Featherstone shared the following:

> Dr. Gustav Eckstein, one of the world's renowned ornithologists, worked in the same laboratory for over 25 years. He bred and crossbred species of birds, and kept meticulous records on the varieties and hybrids of birds in his laboratory. Each day when he would enter

his laboratory he would go down two or three stairs to the stereo. He would put on classical music and turn the volume up very loud. Then he would go about his work. The birds would sing along with the classical music. At the end of the day, about 5:30 P.M., he would turn off the stereo and leave for home.

After 25 years he had to hire a new custodian. One evening after Dr. Eckstein left the laboratory, the new custodian thought the place should be aired out, so he opened all the windows. The next morning when Dr. Eckstein went into his laboratory he saw the open windows and noted that every bird had flown out during the night. He was devastated, his life's work ruined. By habit or instinct, he went to the stereo and turned the classical music up very loud. Then he sat down on the steps, put his head in his hands, and wept.

The strains of music carried out through the open windows, through the trees, and down the streets. In a few moments Dr. Eckstein heard the fluttering of wings. He looked up and saw that the birds were beginning to come back into the laboratory through the open windows. "And," he reported, "every bird came back."

Just as the wayward remnants of the house of Israel will be gathered and acknowledge their God (Mosiah 11:22–23), the wayward children of Israel will also come to realize that the very counsel of wise and loving parents they have rejected in the past is the thing that will ultimately save them. When no one else will stand by them, children will return to the love of family and parents— the very people they once mistrusted and thought intolerant.

It is when we are at the ends of our ropes that God's protecting hand finally becomes the most apparent to us. Often, we can only really come to know and appreciate the power of Christ's Atonement when we see how deep our own weaknesses and inadequacies are. At those times, we realize most poignantly how we depend upon Christ's strength to begin where our efforts end. His enabling power can make up the difference and fill the gaps. When our strength is gone, His strength is perfect. If we give Him an inch, He'll take us a mile. When we feel that we can't carry on, we will feel Him carry us. As difficult and impossible as any situation may seem, He who called Himself the beginning and the end will help us begin wherever we are and make it to the end. The finisher of our faith will help us to the finish line.

Bruce C. Hafen, in his book *The Broken Heart,* writes, "While it is true that no other success of *ours* can fully compensate, there is a success that compensates for all our failures, after all we can do in good faith. That success is the atonement of Jesus Christ." Christ's mercies are suited "according to the conditions of the children of men." (D&C 46:15.) Our background, personal temptations, and individual circumstances are all taken into account. As we repent and try our hardest, Christ will make up the difference. As surely as there is always hope for our teens, there is always hope for us as well. Just as we would light a candle in the window for struggling children, God lovingly lights the way for struggling parents.

Barbara shares the following personal experience in her life because some readers may have a child who has gone astray. Some may have a child that they are really having problems with and they've almost given up on. Hang in there. Some say, "Well, even God lost a third of his children." It is true that many of God's spirit children turned their backs on him, but God never turned his back on them. Those children were lost because they gave up on God and not the other way around. As parents, we must never quit praying, because Heavenly Father will hear us.

Barbara's Story

I was married when I was 19. I married a man who was manic depressive. If you will take the time in your life when you were most depressed and multiply that by one hundred, that's the way my husband used to get.

It wasn't too many months after we were married that I found him on the floor in the bathroom having taken an entire bottle of aspirin. Another time, he took every scrapbook I had made in my life into the backyard and burned them. I thought I could make things better if I had a child. When that little boy was a year and a half old, I was performing in a ballet. My husband called me off-stage and said that there was an emergency. I rushed out to the car, and he put a gag in my mouth, bound my wrists and ankles, and drove off. He had a gun and threatened to kill me. It was horrible.

That was the beginning of a very low time in my life. My mother didn't know anything about what was going on. She just saw the external signs of her daughter deteriorating.

One day, when I couldn't take it anymore, I rushed over to my mother's house with my little boy. I said, "Here, take him. I'm leaving."

I hate to admit it, but I left my son and I ran. I joined the Atlanta Ballet Company. My heart grew hard. I had been through so much trauma and pain with my husband that I never wanted to go home again. My mother, who was Catholic, called every church in El Paso, Texas, and asked them all to pray for her wayward daughter. She called every convent all over the United States and asked them to pray for me.

I didn't know about any of this at the time, but looking back, I see that the prayers of my mother were heard. Several months later, I received a letter from her. She had included a snapshot of my little son with his toy bunny rabbit. I was boarding with a family, and the daughter was playing a music box with the song "Sunrise, Sunset" from *Fiddler on the Roof*.

I set the picture aside and tried to block out the music by reading the newspaper. What I didn't realize was that it was Mother's Day. When I opened the paper I saw this poem:

> "Where are you going?" you'd say to him,
> "And what are you going to do?"
> And with a shy smile, he'd toddle outside
> To slay a dragon for you.
> Or perhaps there was a prince to be,
> Or a lion to track to its lair.
> For a little boy's life is a wondrous thing,
> As long as his mother's there.
> "Why do birds fly all in a flock?
> How far are the stars from the ground?"
> A thousand questions he'd ask of you,
> A thousand answers you found.
> "Please tell me what makes a puppy dog bark?
> And why is the sky filled with air?"
> For a little boy's life is a learning thing,
> As long as his mother's there.
> "Sing me a tune," he'd say to you.
> "Sing me some soft lullabies."

And you'd sit by his bed for a moment or two,
Until slowly he'd close his eyes.
How quiet he'd be as you covered him up,
And caressed his silken hair.
For a little boy's life is a peaceful thing,
As long as his mother's there.
"Don't cry," you'd say as you held him close,
When he'd fallen and hurt his head.
You held back a tear yourself, you know,
When you'd kissed the spot where it bled.
And his tears dried up, and the hurt went away,
Under your gentle care.
For a little boy's life is a loving thing,
As long as his mother's there.
And one day you'll look up, as the years speed by,
And I know it will seem to you
That he isn't a little boy anymore,
But a fine man, grown straight, tall and true.
How fast they go, these little boy years.
Thank God you have them to share.
For though a little boy's life is a fleeting thing,
To a mother, it's always there.

That was a turning point for me. I packed up and went home—home to my mother and home to raise my son. Later, my second husband and I joined the Church. At 19, my son was called to serve his mission to Argentina. On the day of his mission farewell, I recited the above poem. That was the day the poem talked about. I looked up and saw that John wasn't a little boy anymore but a fine man, grown straight, tall, and true.

My Heavenly Father guided me back so I could join the Church with that boy and raise him to serve a mission. Heavenly Father heard the sincere prayers of my mother. I'm grateful she never gave up on me. At a time in my life when things were the darkest, she set her love like a candle in the window, and somehow in the distance I saw the light and came home.

CHAPTER 15

The Solution to Every Problem

The simplest and most direct approach for discipleship is found in filling our minds with thoughts of the Savior, filling our hearts with love of the Savior, and filling our lives with service. Turning young people to the Savior is the best way we can help them through any problem that comes.

"I guess there are things that my parents could do better and I know there are LOTS of things that I could do better. But the bottom line is that my parents have a testimony of the Savior, and they have instilled that in me. So whatever our ups and downs, we love the Savior and we're trying. We'll be okay."

His name was Jack. His nickname was "Jack the Ripper." He was not as big as that name might suggest, but he was that tough. Heaven only knows what got him to the youth conference where we met him. One thing for sure, he didn't want to be there. He ignored most of the activities and wore a face that let everyone know he was bored and distant.

We thought, "How do we reach *this* kid?" We'd almost decided we couldn't. But still, we felt we should try to arrange for our paths to cross. It was more difficult than we imagined. If he came to anything, he was always the last one there and first to leave.

Finally, during one of the meals, Brad saw his chance. Jack had just gotten his plates (yes, *plates,* and no one dared to tell him it was against the rules to take more than one) and sat in the back of the cafeteria away from everyone. Brad quickly got his food and joined him. He didn't ask if he could sit at the same table. He was afraid Jack would say no and break his leg or something.

"Hi!" Brad said. "How are you?"

No response.

"Well, I'm sure hungry. How about you?"

No response.

Brad kept talking, "I'm glad the food is good because I love to eat and that reminds me of something . . . " During the entire meal, Brad carried on a beautiful conversation with the top of Jack's head. Jack never even lifted his eyes or acknowledged his presence. As Jack got close to finishing his food, Brad felt strongly that he needed to reach this young man somehow. "Do you like sports?" he asked.

No response.

"How many in your family?"

No response.

Finally, completely dry of ideas and fishing for anything to say, Brad asked, "So, why do you wear that earring in your ear?"

Jack's head shot up, and he stared at Brad. Had his eyes been a karate move, it would definitely have been black-belt material. He said, "I wear this earring to bug jerks like you."

Brad told himself to stay quiet and let it go. But he felt upset because he had really been trying hard to be nice—and Jack knew it. "Well, Jack," Brad said, "congratulations, you have reached your goal. It does bug me. And I'll tell you why it bugs me. Because you are not only wearing an earring, you are wearing a crucifix, and that is like the cross my Savior was killed on."

Jack pretended not to be listening as he quickly stood and left, banging the door behind him. Several of the adult leaders looked at Brad with puzzled expressions. Things had backfired. After all, the goal of a youth conference is not to drive teenagers out of the Church. Brad picked up his fork and pushed at the cold food he'd been too busy to eat. For one of the few times in his life, he wasn't particularly hungry anymore.

It would be nice to report that Jack came to the rest of the activities with a better attitude or that he bore a tearful testimony at the end of the conference. But he didn't. After the cafeteria episode, he took off and did not come back.

On the Sunday after the conference ended, we had been asked to speak at a special fireside for the deacons and Beehive girls. They had not been able to attend youth conference, and local leaders made it a point that no older youths would be allowed in.

Brad was at the pulpit in the middle of his talk when, at the chapel doors, "Jack the Ripper" appeared. Then Jack sat on the back row and folded his arms. Adult leaders around the room began playing eye-tag back and forth. Their unspoken messages were easy to read: "He's not supposed to be here," "I know, so *you* tell him," "I'm not going to tell him so *you* tell him."

At the pulpit, Brad instantly changed his subject to one about repentance. Now all the young people were listening to words and a testimony that were pointed directly at the young man on the back row who wasn't even supposed to be there.

After the fireside, the 12-and 13-year-olds lined up to greet the speakers. Suddenly Jack stood and started coming forward as well— and he was not about to wait in line behind a bunch of younger kids. He plowed to the front. Brad was scared. They were in a church, surrounded by witnesses, but he knew he had been pretty point-blank with this kid. Would Jack break his legs in a chapel?

As Jack reached the stand, he looked straight at Brad and said, "It's about what you said." Then he reached up to his ear, took off the crucifix, and placed it in Brad's hand. "Now don't you go wearing that"—he smiled slightly—"because that is what they killed my Savior on, and that would really bug me." Brad hugged him.

Everyone has treasured objects—a grandmother's photograph or a mother's wedding ring. We also have small collections of items that mean nothing to anyone else but a great deal to us. One treasure Brad keeps is a single earring—a gold crucifix given to him by a boy named Jack.

Those whose hearts have been turned to Christ are never the same. Anyone who has felt the Spirit of Jesus Christ for even half a minute knows this is true.

The mission of the Church is usually explained by saying, "Preach the Gospel, redeem the dead, and perfect the saints." Too often we overlook the fact that these are not the final goals. They are only the means to the end. Our ultimate mission is to come unto Christ.

Throughout this book, we have suggested ways to help teenagers build their self-esteem and learn about their own self worth, learn to communicate more effectively, deal with pressure and stress, and develop their spirituality. We have offered guiding principles to help parents and leaders keep proper perspectives and positive attitudes as they try to help young people. However, like the threefold mission of the Church, these suggestions are but means to the end. The ultimate goal is to bring ourselves to Christ and then help others, including our teenagers, to find him also.

Low self-esteem vanishes as we draw closer to the Being who

considers us of such infinite worth that He sacrificed everything for us. When teenagers realize their eternal relationship with Christ and their Father in Heaven, they receive a glimpse of who they are and the greatness of their personal earthly missions.

Communication problems can be solved as we more closely emulate the Master. He blessed ears to hear, eyes to see, and the lame to walk. He can bless us with ears to listen, eyes to perceive, and strength to walk in the shoes of others and more truly understand them.

Pressure and stress can be dealt with effectively as we follow him who said, "Come unto me, all ye that labour and are heavy laden, and I will give you rest" (Matthew 11:28), and "In the world ye shall have tribulation: but be of good cheer; I have overcome the world" (John 16:33). Teenagers can seek and find the internal peace of the Savior regardless of the restlessness and harshness of any external circumstance.

Weak testimonies can be strengthened and teenagers can change as they learn to build upon the rock of Christ and not the shifting sand of the world. As young people learn of Christ and keep his commandments, they will be worthy to "always have his spirit to be with them." (Moroni 4:3.) The blessings of safety, companionship, comfort, guidance, and joy can always be theirs.

In our chapters on guiding principles for parents and leaders, we have suggested that keeping perspective, doing our part, and never losing hope are important as we draw closer to the Savior and become more in tune with the will of our Father in Heaven.

Christ is the solution to *every* problem, everywhere, for *everyone*. When He said, "I am the way, the truth, and the life" (John 14:6), He did not qualify Himself or say, "only in certain religious circles where it's not inappropriate to speak of spiritual things."

President Ezra Taft Benson said, "When you choose to follow Christ, you choose the *right* way, the *saving* truth, and the *abundant* life." He didn't add, "unless that contradicts your beliefs and views, offends you or seems extreme in any way." For us and for our teenagers, whatever the problem, drawing closer to Christ is the answer.

On one occasion, we had the marvelous opportunity of presenting firesides in Mexico with Elder and Sister Robert E. Wells. Barbara learned to speak Spanish while growing up on the border in El Paso, Texas, and Brad learned Spanish on his mission to Chile. Now we were having the chance to use that language again.

One morning toward the end of the trip, Barbara was sitting on the patio working on a talk she was preparing for an upcoming Education Days on "Keeping in Tune with the Spirit." Elder Wells was sitting nearby, and Barbara debated whether she should ask him for help. Finally she decided to approach him.

"I'm sorry to interrupt you," she said, "but I'm doing this talk about keeping in tune with the Spirit. Could you give me one or two little pointers?"

Elder Wells smiled and said, "You know, one time we had a meeting of General Authorities at which one of them gave his formula for keeping in tune with the Spirit. I don't think he'd mind if I shared it with you."

Barbara was excited. A General Authority's formula! She smoothed her paper and had her pencil ready to write. And what he said was so simple: "The key to all spirituality is the Savior. Fill your mind with thoughts of the Savior. Fill your heart with love of the Savior. Fill your life with service."

Elder Wells said that the most simple and direct approach for a sincere discipleship of Christ is found in meeting those three challenges.

1. Fill your mind with thoughts of the Savior.

A teenager wrote, "I never used to think about Christ, not even during the sacrament. I guess I figured it wasn't that big a deal. But lately I have been thinking a lot about Him. At school I even thought about Him during a discussion in English. I also thought, 'Now, how would Jesus handle this?' when I was supposed to get a ride home with my friend after volleyball and she forgot and left me stranded. I didn't even get mad, and that's a first for me."

Barbara exercises regularly by walking on a treadmill. Once when Brad visited the Joneses' home, he saw the downstairs room where she works out. On the wall directly in front of the treadmill is a beautiful picture of Christ painted by Gary Kapp. In the tape player she wears as she exercises was Kenneth Cope's tape "Greater Than Us All," with songs about Christ's life. Over the handle of the treadmill were the Book of Mormon and the current issue of the *Ensign*. Brad said, "Even in your exercising, your mind is turned to the Savior." Barbara was quick to say that she needs to do better, but Brad knows that each week when Barbara renews her baptismal covenant to remember Christ *always,* it is not a vacant promise.

2. Fill your heart with love for the Savior.

"After I broke up with my boyfriend last summer I have felt constantly lonely and unwanted," a young woman wrote. "I felt dark and more depressed than ever. How could I feel happy when I felt dead inside? Then last week I went to Temple Square. In the visitors center, I sat down to look at the statue of the Christus because I knew the only comfort I could get would not be on this earth. I said silently in my mind, 'Heavenly Father, do you and

Jesus really love me?' Right then I felt a tap on my shoulder. I turned around and saw Scott, a counselor from the youth programs last summer. He said hello with a big smile and a hug. Right then I knew my prayer was answered. I instantly felt the love of Christ. I have not stopped feeling it all week. I love the Savior so so so so much! I want to help others feel it. It's the greatest feeling on earth."

Our friend Curt Galke has a two-year-old son who embarrasses him regularly. Whenever the boy sees a man with a beard he starts calling out to him, "Jesus! Jesus!" Brad's daughter Whitney is about the same age as Curt's son. When she was just beginning to talk, Brad would often point to the picture of Christ hanging in their home and say, "This is Jesus." Imagine Brad's surprise when he was walking past a display at BYU where there was the same picture of Christ, and Whitney recognized him. She said excitedly, "Jesus!" It was one of her first spoken words.

Brad kept encouraging her to say it over and over. One woman passed and was entranced by how excited Whitney had become over this picture. Brad explained about the picture in his home. The woman said, "Yes, but on the wall in your home was not the first place this child was introduced to Jesus."

Charity is the pure love of Christ. Elder C. Max Caldwell of the Seventy has said the phrase might have meaning in three dimensions: love *for* Christ, love *from* Christ, love *like* Christ.

3. Fill your life with service.

A young man wrote: "When I was a kid, I always loved Kool-Aid to drink, but now I'm learning that the real refresher is not what I take in, but rather what I give out. I call it Cool aid. Like dancing with a girl who doesn't usually get asked, or taking care of some little kids when their folks go to the temple. Once we made cookies and took them to the missionaries' apartment. It was cool—Cool aid. Just saying hello to someone on the street is Cool aid, and the joy I feel lasts a lot longer than the purple mustaches on my upper lip ever did."

Barbara was shocked when Brigham Young University first called to invite her to be a speaker for youth and family programs. She says, "The thing I knew I could never be was a speaker. When it was my turn to read aloud in the third grade, I sniffled and froze. It went that way all through high school. In my senior year, tears streamed down my cheeks while I was presenting an oral book report; my knees shook and my voice quivered." Barbara's first assignment was to speak at a youth conference. She says, "The whole weekend was a nightmare. The young people poured into the classroom wearing jeans and speaking a language I simply didn't comprehend. Needless to say, my talk flopped totally."

That night she went to the dance. She had been advised in her interviews that all speakers should dance with the young people. Brad saw her standing alone and feeling awkward and out-of-place. He picked out a good-looking young man, maneuvered him in Barbara's direction, and said, "David, why don't you ask Sister Jones to dance?"

"Brother Wilcox," David replied with a wince, "my leg is killing me!"

Barbara says, "But the worst blow came when a sweet 18-year-old girl stood up in testimony meeting Sunday morning and, sniffling, said, "I want to th-thank Sister Jones for taking time to t-talk to me last night. I really feel c-close to her, even though (sniff) she is four times my age.' That made me 72!"

Barbara couldn't believe what was happening to her. She

looked up in despair several times and thought, "Heavenly Father, you have made a big mistake if you think I can fit in here!"

But she wanted to serve, so she kept working and kept trying. She learned how to be more effective. When it comes to service, where there's a will there's always a way.

The prophet Alma gave his son Helaman some counsel that confirms what Elder Wells told Barbara: "Let all thy thoughts be directed unto the Lord; yea, let the affections of thy heart be placed upon the Lord forever . . . and he will direct thee for good." (Alma 37:36.) Fill your mind with thoughts of the Savior. Fill your heart with love of the Savior. Fill your life with acts of the Savior.

Chieko Okazaki has written: "To love the Savior with all of our heart, might, mind, and strength doesn't mean that we never think about anything else, never love anyone else, never work at anything else. It means that we think about other things in the presence of the Spirit of Christ. It means that we love others with the same kind of love that he gives us. It means that we work at our daily professions and assignments and Church callings and household chores and offer our good work to the Savior. And making him the center of our hearts enlarges our hearts in wonderful ways. You'll be amazed at how much room there is for other people, for kind words, for swift acts of service, for happy thoughts and gestures when your heart is filled with the love of Jesus."

We testify that Christ lives. His atonement is real. He loves us and leads us today. He truly is the solution to every problem.

CHAPTER 16

"My Opinion Counts"

In this book we wanted teenage voices to be heard. What were the messages we heard most frequently as we compiled the comments of more than one thousand young people?

"I have something to say even though I'm young. In our ward people seem to tune out the youth speakers because they think they aren't saying anything new. Even if that is the case, they are still saying something important."

Who better to talk to parents and leaders about helping young people than young people? When we were preparing our series of Education Week classes for parents on helping teenagers and were also preparing this book for publication, we wanted teenage voices to be heard. We decided to share many of our own personal experiences working with the youth, but we also wanted to share actual words and messages from young people. As we mentioned in the preface, we conducted an informal survey of teenagers by distributing forms that said "Tell your parents how you really feel." Over a thousand teenagers responded.

Some comments were facetious, such as "I wish they would give me a new sports car," or "They should let me stay out all night and not care," or "Hey, this is a switch—me giving *my parents* a lecture for a change! I sure hope they listen to me better than I listen to them!"

The young people were excited about the possibility of telling you things through this book that some of them can't say in person. One of them commented, "It's neat that teenagers are finally going to have a say. I hope my comments can help." Another person wrote, "The things that we teenagers write on these little forms you have given us may not be profound like Socrates or Shakespeare but they are profound in a spiritual sense. They are profound in that they are sincere and coming straight from our hearts. The messages we write on these papers can help to shape, change, and mold eternal relationships. I hope every parent will read these messages, because I know they can make a difference."

Many expressed positive support and appreciation for parents and leaders. Some comments were extremely personal, like an anonymous one in which the teenager wrote a heartbreaking letter about divorce and abuse. Overall, the messages were well thought out, sincere, and insightful—even inspiring. While it's true that kids say the "darnedest" things, we would add that often they say the *deepest* things as well.

We think it would be helpful to summarize the most common bits of advice young people offered to parents and leaders.

The most frequent message, by far, was a plea for trust. The second most common sentiment was a desire for better communication. Other suggestions mentioned frequently dealt with unconditional acceptance, a desire that adults be more involved with in teenagers' lives, and a need to have parents and leaders try harder to live the gospel consistently.

Here are phrases from survey forms that express ideas that surfaced frequently.

"Trust me more."

Treat me like an adult instead of a little kid. Give me space to grow and make my own choices. Let me have some freedom. I won't abuse it. Trust me and don't just expect that I will do the wrong thing. I can make good choices if I'm given the chance. I want ward leaders to stop having a chip on their shoulders about teenagers. Let me have a say in what's happening. Just because you're older doesn't mean you are always right. My opinions count.

Don't forget that I can change. Just because I did something stupid once doesn't mean I will do it again. Give me a chance to start over, and never give up on me—no matter what.

"Let's try to communicate."

Be more understanding. Take time to really listen to what I say and what I feel. Don't lecture all the time or get mad over small things. Don't interrupt when I talk. Remember that sometimes I just want to talk and not get advice. Talk openly and be straightforward and specific. Talk to me about sex and drugs. Offer me suggestions rather than giving me orders. Be quick to praise and slow to criticize.

When I am wrong, correct me in private. I hate it when you lecture me in front of others. Be careful not to reveal my confidences to others in the family or in the ward. Don't always say, "We know what it's like." I don't think you do. Being a teenager now is harder than you realize.

Don't say that what is bothering me isn't important and that adults are the only ones with real problems. My problems are real to me. Don't yell at me. I have an "adult" in me that can be reasoned with. Be careful not to tease me even when you say you are "just kidding."

There are a lot of temptations and problems facing teenagers today. I need to be able to talk about them openly but don't make everything into a serious matter. Lighten up a little and show a sense of humor.

"Accept me for who I am."

Respect me as a person. Tell me, "I love you." I like to hear it and I need to hear it. Give me a hug and don't be afraid to show you love me. Treat me like a friend instead of a child.

Please do not compare me to friends or my brothers and sisters. Treat us all equally and fairly. Playing favorites isn't good for anyone. Accept my individuality. I'm not exactly the same as others just because I'm in the same family or the same church. Be flexible.

Don't complain to your friends about me or tell others about my mistakes. I'm not perfect. I'm learning just like you. Making mistakes is sometimes the only way that I learn. Don't expect me to be perfect, and don't expect me to do something you're not willing to do yourself. Show you love me unconditionally even though you might sometimes be disappointed in what I do. Really care about me and my feelings.

I want my Church leaders to be more like friends and to be with me because they like me and not just because it is a calling. I want ward members to know my name and not just who my parents are. I might be more helpful if I were more appreciated. Notice what I do right, and tell me I'm great and worth more than a million dollars.

"Get involved in my life."

Spend more time together as a family, and don't watch so much TV. I understand that you have to work, but you don't have to work all the time. Do more family activities like going on a picnic or vacation or on special dates one-on-one. Get excited when I'm excited. Show me you care about where I go and what I do. It hurts that you have stopped asking how things are going at school and with my friends. I want to talk about it if you will just listen and not judge.

Be my friend. Come to my activities and meetings. I know you're busy and that my little brothers and sisters need time, but I'm important too. Focus on the positive things I do instead of just the bad things. Don't be afraid to set strict guidelines with me. I like knowing the boundaries. Be there to help me.

"We'll be happier if we try to live the gospel."

Show me the way with your example. Don't teach us one way and act another. Have family home evening and scripture study and family prayers. Talk to us about gospel principles. Pray for us. Don't act one way when the home teachers are there and another way when the family is alone—like putting your arms around me when someone is watching and then swearing at me when they're not.

Show your love for each other more. Share spiritual experiences with the family, and teach me the gospel on a regular basis and not just in Church. I know there are lots of troubles and problems in the world and even in our family, but if we love the Savior and try to follow him together, I know that everything will work out fine.

"Just Help Us See the Savior's Light"

At a youth conference in southern California, we met a hand-some young man named Hector. During the conference we gave him one of our survey forms and asked him to fill it out. He read the instructions and then said, "No, I can't do this."

"Come on," we encouraged him, "we would love to read what you have to say."

"No, I don't know what I'd write."

"Come on."

He was still hesitant. "There are lots of other teenagers here. You can find someone else."

Brad said, "We'll give forms to them too, but we really do want to know what you think. What is *your* message?"

He finally took the paper and said, "I don't really have anything to say, but I'll try."

As the congregation was singing the opening hymn at the concluding session of the conference, a testimony meeting, we were sitting toward the front of the chapel when someone tapped Brad on the shoulder and passed a folded note.

While everyone around us continued singing, we unfolded the paper. It was the survey form from Hector. As we read his words, we were touched deeply. This teenager who didn't have "anything to say" really said it all:

> A teenage world is difficult,
> It's full of darkness, pain, and sin.
> There's pressure from both friends and foes
> Which causes confusion deep within.
> At times you want to get away
> And just be all alone.

That's when you need your parents there
To calm you when the storms have blown.
Parents, leaders, please remember this:
For us each day is like a fight.
When teenagers are in the dark,
Just help us see the Savior's light.
—Hector Lopez

May our Lord and Savior, Jesus Christ, bless you as you strive to bring his children back home to him. We love you, and we love your youth.

Sources

Ballard, M. Russell. "Purity Precedes Power." *Ensign,* November 1990.

Barlow, Brent J. *Twelve Traps in Today's Marriage and How to Avoid Them.* Salt Lake City: Deseret Book, 1986.

Britsch, R. Lanier, and Terrance D. Olson. *Counseling: A Guide to Helping Others.* 2 vols. Salt Lake City: Deseret Book, 1983,1985.

Caldwell, C. Max. "Love of Christ." *Ensign,* November 1993.

Cope, Kenneth. "Hear Them Cry." *Voices.* Midvale, Utah: Embryo-Music Co., 1991.

Featherstone, Vaughn J. *A Generation of Excellence.* Salt Lake City: Bookcraft, 1975.

Featherstone, Vaughn J. *Charity Never Faileth.* Salt Lake City: Deseret Book, 1980.

Finding the Light in Deep Waters and Dark Times: Favorite Talks from Especially for Youth. Salt Lake City: Bookcraft, 1992.

High Fives and High Hopes: Favorite Talks Especially for Youth. Salt Lake City: Deseret Book, 1990.

Holland, Jeffrey R., and Patricia T. Holland. *On Earth As It Is in Heaven.* Salt Lake City: Deseret Book, 1989.

Lundberg, Joy Saunders. "It's a Date." *Ensign,* June 1992.

Okazaki, Chieko N. *Cat's Cradle.* Salt Lake City: Bookcraft, 1993.

Okazaki, Chieko N. *Lighten Up!* Salt Lake City: Deseret Book, 1993.

Packer, Boyd K. *Let Not Your Heart Be Troubled.* Salt Lake City: Bookcraft, 1991.

Sharing the Light in the Wilderness: Favorite Talks from Especially for Youth. Salt Lake City: Deseret Book, 1993.

Smith, Joseph. *History of the Church.* 7 vols. plus index. Salt Lake City: Deseret Book.

"The New Teens." *Newsweek,* Fall/Winter 1990.

Top, L. Brent, and Bruce A. Chadwick. "The Power of the Word: Religion, Family, Friends, and Delinquent Behavior." *BYUStudies* 33:2 (Spring 1993).

Wells, Robert E. *The Mount and the Master.* Salt Lake City: Deseret Book, 1991.

Widtsoe, John A., ed. *Discourses ofBrigham Young.* Salt Lake City: Deseret Book, 1954.

About the Authors

Barbara Barrington Jones and Brad Wilcox, who relate well to both teenage and adult audiences, are popular speakers at youth conferences, Especially for Youth, and Education Week programs, and other Church gatherings.

Barbara, a native of Texas, is a convert to The Church of Jesus Christ of Latter-day Saints. As a nationally recognized image consultant, she has helped many young women to prepare for—and win—beauty pageants, including five contestants from Texas who became Miss USA. She and her husband, Hal, who reside in California's Bay area, have two children.

Brad Wilcox, a graduate of Brigham Young University, received a Ph.D. in education from the University of Wyoming and is an assistant professor in the College of Education at BYU. He has served as a member of the national executive board of Boy Scouts of America and served a mission to Chile. He and his wife, the former Debi Gunnell, have four children.